Hidden Holiness:
Voices of Priests

by
Thomas A. McCabe

To Katie,
Thanks for your
encouragement in getting
this book published.
Peace,
(Tom & Eileen)

Hidden Holiness: Voices of Priests

Cover design by Liz Sullivan and Daniel Sullivan

Printed and bound in the United States of America

McCabe, Thomas A.

Hidden Holiness: Voices of Priests

ISBN 0-9799390-0-3

1. Research   2. Religion

Dedicated to Father Thomas Mannion whose love of beauty led him to plant and nourish a garden in each of his assignments in Brooklyn and Gold Beach, Oregon. The garden is a symbol of the man himself who loved diversity and who nourished the spirit of those around him with his goodness and faith.

Many thanks to my good friend, Vincent Murphy, for walking with me through many revisions of *Hidden Holiness* over the past two years. He always responded with insight and good humor.

Thanks also to David Gawlik, my editor, publisher and friend for his patience, advice and timely response to my many requests.

Table of Contents

IV

Table of Contents

Hidden Holiness: Voices of Priests

From 1960 to 1970 Tom McCabe was a priest in St. Ann's parish in the Diocese of Brooklyn. Along with Fr. Tom Mannion and Fr. Gerry Gannon they developed a team ministry as they served the people in the Farragut Housing Projects. Their innovative Liturgies attracted people from all over the city.

A turning point for Tom was his response to the call of Dr. Martin Luther King to join in the struggle for civil rights in Selma, Alabama. Tom realized that voting rights and peace are Gospel issues, not just political issues.

When Tom left the active ministry, he married Eileen Dowd, a former Sister of St. Joseph. Together they have four children and five grandchildren.

For the next 25 years Tom taught and supervised Special education classes in NYC while being one of the founders of the Renewal Coordinating Community (RCC) and Voice of the Ordained (VOTO).

Much of his time now is spent teaching ESL to day laborers in the Jornaleros program and working with Helping Hands, an organization that provides shelter in communities of faith for homeless people in Rockland County.

Hidden Holiness: Voices of Priests

CHAPTER ONE

The Project

PURPOSE

As the sexual abuse charges were being made public by the Boston Globe and other newspapers throughout the country, a group of priests held an informal meeting in St. Barbara's rectory in the Bushwick section of Brooklyn. As a married priest of the Diocese of Brooklyn, I was invited. As we searched for an appropriate action we could take to show our support both for the victims of sexual abuse and priests who have been wrongfully accused, I realized I was in the presence of good men, not perfect by any means but good, caring and humble men who were trying to do the right thing. Yet, we hardly ever hear from them. We don't know their stories.

This book is written with a clear focus: to listen to the stories of a few priests, some of whom may be living heroic lives, but whose stories we never hear. Most of us are tired of hearing the stories of the "bad guys" in newspapers and TV talk shows. We'd like to hear the stories of some of the "good guys" for a change. We will listen to what they have to say, in their own words, about their priesthood, celibacy, voluntary poverty, what they are most proud of, the future of the Church, the next generation of priests, prayer, living alone, friendships and intimacy in their lives. It is also about history.

METHODOLOGY

The methodology used in this book is that of case studies. It does not pretend to be a scientific study of the Catholic priesthood whose results can be applied to a larger population beyond those who took part in the study. Questionnaires were not filled out. The priests in this study represented themselves, not all priests. This does not make their stories less important. On the contrary, the opinions and stories of the priests in this study, gathered in face-to-face conversation, carry with them an authenticity and a sense of reality that the more structured sociological studies cannot capture. Surveys are good. They appeal to our intellect. They are analytical. Case studies are good. They appeal to our emotions. They are stories. Here are some examples:

It is one thing for a recent survey of 1300 priests to report that 42% felt overwhelmed by the amount of work they had to do. It is another thing to hear Frank Shannon, the sole priest serving what was at one time four parishes, say, "To be the pastor of more than one parish is a recipe for burnout. Each of the parishes is big and I'm the only priest. Each church has 600-700 people on a Sunday morning. Each one has 200 kids in CCD programs. Each has a separate budget and a separate Church bulletin. The administrative work of being the pastor of inner-city churches is overwhelming."

Or again. It is one thing to read in a survey that only 38% of priests feel that the morale of their fellow priests is good. It is another thing to hear Richard Smith say, "We have a serious problem in this diocese; namely, the lack of priestly fraternity. We don't reach out to each other. We are very divided and our divisions are rooted in fear."

PARTICIPANTS

Participants were all interviewed and their responses recorded on an audio cassette tape. Most of the interviews were conducted in the rectory where the priests were living. Each interview lasted about an hour- and- a- half to two hours. If clarification was needed, a second interview was set up, focusing on the issues that needed clarification.

In all, 15 priests were interviewed, 14 celibate priests and one married priest. I began with two priests who had been present at the meeting in Brooklyn. They in turn recommended others who in turn recommended others. Some of the priests I knew. Others I was meeting for the first time. Two priests declined to be interviewed.

From the very beginning I thought it was important that we hear each man's story and that we hear it in his own words.

My role became that of editor, that is, to take what might have been, at first, a rambling discourse and make it a more concise and readable story without losing the spirit and fire and vocabulary of the original.

I was impressed with the openness of the priests. They did not question me or my motives. There was no talk of a "hidden agenda," nor a lot of questions asking "why are you doing this?" I did not sense any reluctance to criticize bishops or the Vatican. The men seemed to be free.

My overall impression was that people tried to be honest. They did not seem to care about the political consequences of what they had to say. They were actually grateful for the chance to talk about their ministry and their own personal lives. They found the interviews unique in the sense that no one from the bishop's office or even fellow priests were asking them how they were doing and how their ministry was progressing, and here I was asking them intimate questions about ministry, celibacy and their bishop.

Some expressed gratitude that the interview made them reflect on themselves and their work. They seemed pleased that someone was actually interested in what they had to say.

THE FOLLOWING PRIESTS WERE INTERVIEWED AND RECORDED:

BRYAN KARVELIS spent 50 years in the same parish in Williamsburg, Brooklyn, working with immigrants. When he needed a kidney transplant, one of his parishioners donated his kidney. For years Bryan has given over the rectory as a shelter for 25 to 30 homeless men while he lived in an apartment. Bryan died on October 18, 2005. Many of those who knew him and recognized that his work with the poorest came from a deep prayer life, consider him to be a saint and a saint for our time. Excerpts from a newspaper article in the *New York Daily News* concerning Bryan's 50- year ministry can be found at the end of his interview.

BOB VITAGLIONE has become such an expert on Immigration Law that he is recognized as an "Immigration Lawyer." Over a 25- year ministry he has been able to defend and save thousands of immigrants from being deported.

JOHN POWIS has spent his life dealing with issues of housing and education. He is one of the founders of an ecumenical social action organization called East Brooklyn Congregations. EBC has built over 3,000 affordable single- family homes in Brooklyn's inner-city. EBC also sponsors and supervises two high schools approved by the New York City Board of Education. John had a leadership role in the "experimental parish'" that was Our Lady of the Presentation. He is retired and working on his new idea which he calls "Church without walls."

ANDY CONNOLLY, a priest in the Diocese of Rockville Center, spent 17 years in a mission in the Dominican Republic working on such basic issues as waste disposal and the availability of clean water. He is a recovering alcoholic. Excerpts from "A Letter to God from an Alcoholic" can be found at the end of his interview.

FRANK SHANNON was made the pastor of two parishes that had already merged with two other parishes. This means that he is the sole priest ministering to the needs of the people in what used to be four parishes.

JOE DIELE spends three to four hours in prayer and study each day. On most Sundays he preaches to his Black congregation for 35 to 40 minutes and most of them come back the following Sunday! Joe took a leave from active ministry in the Roman Catholic Church a few months after completing this interview. He joined the Catholic Apostolic Church in North America (CACINA), but he now feels even that is too structured. "You don't need a structure to preach the Gospel," he said. He continues to do a great deal of retreat work and give spiritual direction. He has been ex-communicated by Bishop DiMarzio, the Bishop of Brooklyn.

JIM RICHARDSON works among the poor in New Haven, Connecticut. He is a member of the Sons of Charity, a religious order that grew out of the Priest-Worker movement in France after World War II.

JOHN MULHERN is married with three children. He served as a priest for five-and-a-half years in Transfiguration parish in Williamsburg, Brooklyn. He married Luz, a parishioner of Transfiguration where they continue to live and have raised three children. John has remained so active in the parish and the community that some parishioners still call him "Padre Juan."

BILL BRISOTTI was greatly influenced by Dorothy Day and the Catholic Worker movement. He was suspended by his bishop because he chose not to live in the rectory, but instead to live with the poor in a Catholic Worker house of hospitality located in the parish. Bill used the time of his suspension to broaden his work for peace and justice particularly by participating in several acts of civil disobedience at the Pentagon resulting in short periods of jail time. He also visited refugee camps in El Salvador to show solidarity between North and Central America.

RICHARD SMITH is a priest of the Archdiocese of New York. Along with his regular parish duties, which include a growing and successful youth ministry, he is studying for a doctorate in Theology at Fordham University. Being a young priest himself, he tried to articulate the positions and concerns of some of the "next generation of priests." Richard was extremely upset by the Dallas Charter that blamed priests for sexual abuse, but did not blame any bishop for trying to cover up the scandal. He was ordained in 1997. In May he was assigned to a new parish, St. Margaret's in Pearl River, and then to Annunciation in Crestwood.

JACK PEYTON lived alone for ten years in a community center in Brownsville, Brooklyn, where he developed a ministry to an expanding Haitian Community. This required that he speak not only English and Spanish, but French and Creole as well. He now is the pastor of the parish with the only thriving Catholic school in the East New York section of Brooklyn.

JOE NUGENT is now the pastor of Our Lady of the Presentation parish in Brownsville. For over 20 years he directed a very successful shelter for addicts and he did so without any government money. As he himself admits, it was in this shelter, where he slept every night with addicts, that he learned what it means to be a priest.

DONALD KENNA was both a parish priest and a Priest-Worker for 21 years. During this time he said Mass, preached and baptized. He also worked in the billing department at Con Edison. Most of this time he lived alone in an apartment in Brooklyn. Sadly, Don died of a massive heart attack on June 6, 2006.

JIM SULLIVAN founded the Religious Consultation Center to provide counsel and therapy for priests and sisters, many of whom were in crisis. Celibate himself, he was very active in the movement for optional celibacy for priests and he wrote extensively on this subject. He died in 2006 after being a priest for 60 years.

JOHN GILDEA spent many years in South America and Central America in parishes supported by the Diocese of Brooklyn. He requested to return home rather than live alone when it became clear that no other priest was going to join him. He was made the pastor of merged parishes as he fought his own battle with cancer. He now has a new assignment in a parish that is not merged and has only one building that has to be maintained.

ORAL HISTORY

History is usually written from the viewpoint of the leaders of the time being studied. So a history of the Catholic Church in the 20th century would be a history of the popes and influential bishops of that time, what they said and what they did, their failings and their successes.

Oral history is very different. It is more like a memory book. It is an effort to hear the stories of the average citizen, the "person in the street," people who lived in a particular time and place. It is done in the tradition of Studs Terkel who told the story of the great depression, not from the point of view of the union president or the secretary of labor, but from the point of view of the coal miner and the unemployed factory worker.

Hidden Holiness is in this tradition of Oral History as it attempts to see Church history from the 1960's to the present time, not from the viewpoint of those who were popes or bishops, but from the viewpoint of some priests who lived and ministered to people during that time and whose stories have never been heard.

The interviews presented in this book follow in the tradition of Oscar L. Arnal who wrote a history of the Worker-Priest movement in his book, *Priests in Working Class Blue*. Arnal set for himself the clear but difficult task to "recreate and portray the very stuff of the lives and the priesthood of the Worker-Priests. What they were and what they are, what they did and what they experienced deserves to be told in all its richness." In order to accomplish his goal Arnal interviewed as many of the original Worker-Priests that he could find. He wanted to hear their stories before they died with the "richness" of their stories dying with them.

This is also a concern in this book. There is a "richness" in the stories of the priests who consented to share their experiences. Since this project began, three priests haves died, two have retired, and one has left the active ministry in the Catholic Church. If we do not record these stories now, they may be lost forever.

I would like to end on a personal note. For me it was a privilege to listen to the stories of these priests who are unknown outside of a small circle of parishioners and co-workers. They are some of the "good guys" whose stories do not get told unless we go out of our way to get them. I hope the reader will be inspired by these stories and enjoy reading them as much as I did in recording them. The book has no "hidden agenda." Hopefully it speaks for itself.

Thomas A. McCabe

Tom McCabe was ordained for the Diocese of Brooklyn in 1960 and served in the Diocese for ten years. In 1970 he married Eileen Dowd, a former Sister of St. Joseph. They have four children and five grandchildren. Tom worked in New York City Public Schools for 25 years. For seven years he directed the TORCH (To Reach Children) program for pre-school handicapped children under the auspices of the Dominican Sisters of Blauvelt. He is one of the founders of The Renewal Coordinating Community (RCC). He has been involved in Church renewal activities for 30 years.

CHAPTER TWO

REV. WILLIAM F. BRISOTTI

PEACEMAKER

I have spent most of my priesthood in peace work and in parish work.

I was ordained from the Seminary in Huntington, Long Island, for the Diocese of Rockville Center in 1968 and I was assigned to Our Lady of Loretto in Hempstead. I was there for six years until 1974. Then I came here to Wyandanch for the next 30 years. Andy Connolly was already here when I came. He had just been made the administrator. There was an older priest also assigned here at this time. He was sick and was not living here. Technically he was considered the pastor, but he was an absentee pastor. Andy was the administrator and

I was the assistant. We worked together until 1983 when Andy left to refresh his Spanish and to go to the Dominican Republic. I was here alone and I've been alone ever since.

Andy was told to find someone he could work with. It was rather unique, of course, that they would allow Andy to look for an assistant outside of the usual assignment process. Andy asked around and got the names of a few people who "might be crazy enough" to go to Wyandanch and work with him. He called me on the Feast of Our Lady of Guadalupe. I was not getting along with the priests in the rectory. The pastor and I did not see eye-to-eye on any issue. I was frustrated. Andy called and asked me if I wanted to go to Wyandanch. I had been at Our Lady of Loretto for six years and I was due to be transferred anyway. So now I had some options. I wanted to work with Afro-Americans and Latinos. This gave me the opportunity and I took it. I was ready for a change. The letter of transfer came in a few days. I had started a Spanish Mass at Loretto. The diocese found a priest who had done some work in Peru. He took my place and continued the Spanish Mass. When they want to, the diocese can move quickly.

There was a lot of tension in the rectory at Loretto and I was glad to leave it behind me and start anew. For example, the town was trying to integrate the fire department. Many people objected to it and tensions were high. The "senior curate" in the parish told me to mind my own business and stay away from it all. He referred to Martin Luther King as a "trouble maker." On the other hand, I was speaking out about justice and attending demonstrations favoring integration. There was almost as much tension in the rectory as there was in the community.

I had studied Spanish for two years in high school without any thought I would actually use it. Then in 1963, while still a seminarian, a group of us decided to spend the summer in Latin America with Maryknoll in Peru.

So I went from not seeing a need for Spanish to getting ready to spend a summer in Peru. Actually, I spent three summers working with Maryknoll in Peru and Chile building homes and coops. Also we found an unused room in the Seminary and we set it up as a "language lab." We had the "Spanish Made Simple" tapes and a tape recorder. It was pretty simple but it worked.

I had come to love the Spanish language and I wanted to learn it well and speak it as well as I could. I remember that when I spent the summers with Maryknoll, one of their priests used verbs in the infinitive only and he had been in Peru for 20 years. I didn't want to speak Spanish like that. I never went to the Spanish Institute. I wish now that I had taken the time to go but I never did.

I always wanted to work with the poor. Even before I knew anything about the Catholic Worker, I envisioned the priest as one who works with the poor. Gradually the idea clarified and became more focused. When I was in high school, I spent my summers on Long Island farms and I met Hispanic farm workers from Puerto Rico. I rode my bike to work each morning and worked with Puerto Rican farm workers during the day. I found out that they were paid 75 cents per hour and I was being paid $1.00 an hour. Here I was a high school kid making more per hour than those who were supporting families in Puerto Rico. I was struck by the injustice in the system.

I attribute my involvement in the peace and justice movement to my family, to my parents in particular. They were always politically involved as we were growing up in Glen Cove here on the Island. We came from the Bronx but moved to Glen Cove when I was three. One of my earliest and strongest memories about my parents centered around the execution of Julius and Ethel Rosenberg. I knew from my parents' conversations how very wrong this was and I was only eleven. My parents were convinced that the Rosenbergs would not be executed. They were not involved in any anti-death penalty movement but I would hear them talking about the immorality of capital punishment. My parents always voted and were always very politically aware. A lot of their values rubbed off on me. My parents were devastated when the Rosenbergs were executed. I identified with the Rosenberg children since they were around my age. I did meet them later on. They were very active against capital punishment.

I also admired my grandfather who was a dean at Chelsea Vocational High School in New York City. It is still there. If I were off from school, I'd go over to "grandpa's school" and spend the day there. My grandfather worked with tough New York City students. He tried to help them and orientate them to the future. He was a very open man and he had an influence on me.

In Christmas of 1962, I was in the seminary and I heard that a Jesuit priest was going to be speaking over in Central Islip and a few of us decided that since we were on vacation we would go. Father Charlie Kohli set it up for us. We went to the talk and I was impressed by the priest, Father Dan Berrigan. He talked about the war in Indochina and the injustices perpetrated by our government around the world. I started to get involved in the peace movement. My father would send me articles he'd cut out of the newspapers. (Remember we were not permitted to bring newspapers into the Seminary or listen to the radio in those days.) My father was a great reader of newspapers and he would keep me up to date on what was happening in the world.

14

I joined the "Long Island Catholic Peace Fellowship" in 1966 and later "Pax Christi Long Island." I was involved in draft counseling during the Vietnam War and I was a supporter of conscientious objectors. I was introduced to Dorothy Day at the Catholic Worker around this time. When I could, I would visit the Worker, especially on Friday nights, to hear a lecture and join in the discussion. I began to get the Catholic Worker Newspaper and cut out the Fritz Eichenberg pictures from the front cover and paste the pictures around the room. I used to be very involved in the peace movement. I'm not as involved as I once was.

In my most active years I made numerous trips to Central America, especially to El Salvador during the 1980's, sponsored by organizations such as "Witness for Peace."

I've been an active member of the "Atlantic Life Community" since 1977. It's a union of faith-based peace communities from Maine to North Carolina supporting each other in direct nonviolent action for disarmament. It was founded by Phil Berrigan and his wife, Liz McAlister.

I've participated in several acts of nonviolent civil disobedience at the Pentagon and I've been jailed for short periods of time.

I'm a member of "Pastors for Peace" challenging the United States embargo against Cuba.

I was involved in 2001 in the rebuilding of communities in El Salvador following a series of devastating earthquakes.

I could give you other examples but I'm sure you get a flavor of my activities with various peace groups.

The call to work for peace comes at Baptism. Baptism is the fundamental sacrament of initiation into Christ and membership in the Church. Priesthood defines a role within that community, a role of leadership. People talk about the peace gospel or the social gospel. What other Gospel is there? Is there a non-peace gospel or a non-social gospel? I don't think so. I don't see how one can read the Gospel and read about Jesus who is such a non-violent person and still support war and violence. Jesus was clearly a peace maker and a challenger of unjust structures.

Priests who participate in public demonstrations will often get the publicity. This is not bad. The role of the priest is a leadership role. He must use it for others. He must use his prestige for the good of others. It would be false humility for a priest to deny that he has a leadership role.

I think the "immersed in community" model of priest is the model I try to follow. It is the kind of leader I want to be. It requires a commitment to "be there." I remember Msgr. Jim Coffey, a profound leader and intellectual, re-thinking his philosophy and theology as he got older. He used to see priesthood as the culmination of the Christian life. But now he sees baptism as the foundation. I remember him saying, "I am first of all a man (birth), then I am a Christian (Baptism), and then a priest (Holy Orders.)" You can not understand the priesthood outside of the call to follow Christ at Baptism.

I remember William Sloan Coffin saying that those in the highest positions of authority are usually the farthest away from the people. This is the opposite of immersion. Very often as people move into positions of authority they become more isolated; for example, a bishop who does not know his priests or his people and makes no effort to get to know them. He doesn't mingle with them. I've always believed the more you talk with people the better your chances of making good decisions. I go to many meetings around here just to listen to people and to let them know I'm available.

What does worry me is the younger priests that I've met or heard about. I am very nervous about younger priests. At priest meetings I'd bring up issues of peace and the younger priests would often voice opposition, not just a lack of interest but opposition, to peace and justice issues.

The younger priests that I see and talk with feel that the fundamental role of the priest is the moral formation of the laity. It is a different vision. I had a recent experience at a deanery meeting. I raised the point about the divisions that exist in our diocese. As priests of the diocese we should be concerned about these divisions and what we can do to heal them and get the dialogue going between the bishop and Voice of the Faithful if there is to be any hope of resolving the conflict about using Church property for VOTF meetings. One of the younger priests responded to me as if I were his altar boy. He said he understood how emotional I was about these issues. He was condescending and patronizing. I was 36 years ordained and he was talking down to me. What arrogance! I've seen it many times. The young priests feel they have the answers. They have their package of truth that the people must accept. They have studied theology so the people must listen to them. Some of them seem to feel that priests who have been formed in a pastoral approach have been poorly trained. Walking a picket line or demonstrating for peace in Iraq is the farthest thing from their minds. They have the package of truth from the pope and the bishops. The role of the laity is to accept everything that is in the package. We (clerics) have the answers. Our job is to teach the laity, not to learn from them.

They see organizations like VOTO (Voice of the Ordained) or VOTF as divisive and therefore wrong and harmful even though Jesus said, "I did not come to bring peace but division." Sometimes division is needed for clarification and understanding. The young priests go along with whatever the bishop says.

The big issue surrounding the priesthood today is the shortage of priests and does mandatory celibacy contribute to this shortage. I'd like to talk about this.

I've always believed in optional celibacy. Celibacy should be optional. I don't know whether I would have chosen it if I had the opportunity to marry. I don't go there. I look at my brothers with their families at family functions. I'm the odd-ball uncle out there. They wonder what picket line I'm going to be on or what country I'll be in. At least with a cell phone and e-mail they can always reach me. I look at classmates of mine who left the Catholic priesthood, married and are now Episcopal priests. I'm thinking of people like Gerry Gallagher and Bill Viola. I definitely think optional celibacy is good for the priesthood. Mandatory celibacy has been hurtful to some priests. I've seen it. I've seen good people destroyed by mandatory celibacy. I think that in order to compensate for the lack of wife and family some priests have buried themselves in things, in materialism. Intimacy is important in life. Sometimes I wonder what my life would have been like if I had pursued a relationship with a woman I've met along the way and with her still keep the commitments I feel so strongly about, especially being involved in the peace movement and in the Catholic Worker. I think of Tony and Mary Equale. There is no valid reason he is still not an active priest. The Church has missed a lot.

Another thing I have seen is that in Protestant Churches new ministers often come from families where the father is a minister. I often think how different things would be if we had married priests and they had sons and daughters. I think of the founder of Pastors for

Peace. His daughter is dynamic and a leader in justice and peace efforts. I look at Phil Berrigan and Liz McAlister and their three children – all involved in the peace movement and in the Catholic Worker. I might have been involved, like them, in some kind of an urban community, if I had married.

Celibacy, of course, is not the only issue in today's priesthood. Poverty does not get the kind of publicity that celibacy gets, but it is very important. It has gotten me into a lot of trouble. In 1983 I founded a Catholic Worker house of hospitality as a shelter and sanctuary for undocumented refugees from Central America right here in Wyandanch. I wanted to live in community in the house and continue to serve in the parish. Bishop McGann was opposed to this. I could have done it quietly and just moved out of the rectory and lived in the house of hospitality. He would not have known. He never came to visit the parish, except for one confirmation. Anyway, I let him know what I was doing and I was suspended from the priesthood in 1983 for not obeying his directive to move back into the rectory

A group of us had pooled our resources and bought a house that needed a lot of work a few blocks from the Church. The place was a mess. We had to rebuild it. We began to offer it as hospitality to undocumented immigrants. Since I was suspended for living in the House of Hospitality, I used my time to get more involved in Latin America. I lived in a refugee camp in El Salvador for a while and did other things in other Central American countries as the needs arose.

But getting back to my feelings about the importance of poverty: I think poverty is a charism, a very important charism for a priest and for all who want to be disciples of Jesus. Voluntary poverty becomes a charism when a person has a strong urging not to depend on material things but to depend on God. It is important for all of us to use our resources for the common good and not to save it for the "rainy days" ahead. It is disturbing for me to see priests acquiring properties. I don't want to judge others but it distresses me to see priests buying vacation homes and/or retirement homes. And these are good guys that I respect doing this. Voluntary poverty has always been a challenge for me. I try to be generous in distributing my resources.

I try to give away as much of my money as I can. I own a car. I own some musical instruments. I play the banjo and I play in a traditional Irish band. (Music has always been a part of me and a part of my ministry.) I have a collection of musical instruments. I enjoy them and I play various instruments. But there is always the temptation for me and for all of us to acquire more than we need. This is where poverty comes in. There is a line between acquiring what we need but not more than we need. I channel my resources in particular ways depending on needs. The parish here in Wyandanch has a relationship with the diocesan mission in the Dominican Republic. We send money down there on a regular basis. Most of my money goes into these projects.

I finally decided to leave the House of Hospitality and return to the parish. I came to see that I could do more good as a priest in the parish than living outside the parish. Henri Nouwen was a big influence in helping me make my decision. I returned to the rectory and the suspension was lifted. It was a win-win situation. It was good for me and good for the parish that I return to the rectory.

I lead a very hectic life as pastor of this parish with no other priest here. But I know I have to make time to pray and be disciplined about it. Prayer for me is quiet time, focusing on a particular passage from scripture, maybe the coming Sunday readings, trying to keep out distractions, trying to use centering prayer. My prayer time tends to be either early in the morning or late at night. I found it easier to pray in the rectory or in the Church rather than in the Catholic Worker house. There I had to get out of the house and go to the park in order to find peace and quiet.

I try to get in 20 to 30 minutes of this focused prayer each day. The Breviary was never for me – too formal. Very often my prayer during the week leads to a homily preparation. I do not want to lose touch with prayer. It is very important for me and my ministry.

I'm known as a peace person and I'm proud of that. I feel guilty about not spending more time with the youth. They are open, not always looking for religion but looking for spirituality. I don't think the Catholic high schools out here teach peace. A lot of kids are conflicted because of the war in Iraq. Maybe I'll try to become more active in the local Catholic high school and do some counseling or teach a class on peace. We'll see.

CHAPTER THREE

REV. ANDREW P. CONNOLLY

MISSIONARY TO THE POOR

I was ordained a priest in 1956 for the Diocese of Brooklyn. So I've been a priest for 50 years. They have been good years, difficult but good. Most of these years, except for my first assignment, were spent in poor parishes. When I was ordained, I had hoped to work with Puerto Ricans in Brooklyn, but instead, I was assigned to the richest parish in the Diocese of Brooklyn, St. Agnes in Rockville Centre. But even that was a good experience. I learned a lot of things through this experience and I made contacts with people I would not have met if I had not been assigned to St. Agnes. It changed many things in my life. Instead of working in the inner city my whole life long, I ended up doing things I never would have done. I learned about affordable housing and urban renewal. I saw how many Whites spoke about Blacks and acted towards Black people. I learned about segregation when Bishop Kellenberg assigned me to be the Assistant Chaplain to the Catholic Interracial Council. It was, again, a good experience for me, one I would not have had if I were not in St. Agnes.

I am convinced of the need to work with the poor from Jesus' own words. The proof that he is the Messiah is that "the blind see, the lame walk and the poor have the Gospel preached to them." I remember clearly coming across this verse in the seminary and it hit me: "Of course! That is the way it has to be." It is our job, clear and simple, to preach the Gospel to the poor. Most of the time I have been able to do that. Even when I was working in the richest parish in the diocese, at that time, I was able to use the Spanish I had taught myself. And I worked with a large Black community, very poor, in the middle of this rich parish. Working with the poor has shaped my life.

It goes back to when I was a kid. I grew up in a normal middle-class Catholic family in Middle Village, Queens. We were not rich, neither were we very poor. My father had a steady job. We did not have a lot of things but we did ok. I went to the normal middle-class Catholic school with all sorts of middle-class and upper-middle-class values taught to me. Some of which were very good.

I was an activist, even as a little kid. At the age of 14 I belonged to a group called the Christian Front. No one has ever heard of it. It was a Nazi organization, extremely right wing. Even at the age of 14 I used to distribute literature in Manhattan for the Christian Front. I would attend Christian Front rallies. I was surrounded by right-wing values both politically and economically. At 14 years of age I did not understand much of this, but there was something there that attracted me.

I graduated from Catholic elementary school and went to Bishop Loughlin High School in downtown Brooklyn. I rode the bus and subway every day. I remember very distinctly sometime in May, several months before my 15th birthday, I came across an issue of the Catholic Worker. I said to myself, "The Catholic Worker? What is this all about?" I brought it home and read it cover to cover. It struck me that it did not mention most of what I had learned in Catholic schools. It was all about voluntary poverty and peace in the midst of war. (Remember, we were still fighting WW II.) There was a lot of material about conscientious objectors. I wondered what all of this had to do with the Catholic Church. I was attracted to it, but I did not understand it at all.

Just by coincidence I happened to be in Incarnation Church in Bellerose. They had a pamphlet rack at the rear of the Church and I saw a pamphlet by Msgr. John K. Ryan entitled, "The Christian Doctrine of Poverty." I had never heard of Msgr. John K. Ryan, but I found out later that he was a giant in spreading the Church's social doctrine. I can still remember a quote from St. Augustine on the cover of the pamphlet, "The superfluities of the rich are the necessities of the poor." That made such good sense to me. I was never taught that in school. It was a well kept secret.

So here we are in June, 1945. School was ending and vacations beginning. I was still not quite 15 years old. I asked for and received permission from my parents to visit the Catholic Worker in downtown Manhattan. I went there and quickly met, of all people, the founder of the Catholic Worker, Dorothy Day. In my first meeting with Dorothy she did not say "hello" or "good-by." She did not greet me at all. Instead she said, "Thank God you're here. We need someone over there to make sandwiches." These were her first words to me. I can remember them clearly. So that is what I would do when I went to the Catholic Worker: I made sandwiches. Little by little I got to know Dorothy and it just radically altered my life. It challenged the whole

25

direction of my life. Meeting her, going to the Worker, seeing her work with the poor changed me.

Through Dorothy and the Catholic Worker, I got to know Baroness de Hueck Doherty and Friendship house in Harlem. For the first time in my life I met Black people on a one-to-one basis. I had grown up in a family where Blacks were called "niggers" and Jews were called "Kikes." I grew up with the normal prejudices that anyone in my situation would have grown up with. But now my contact with Blacks on a one-to-one basis really turned me around, completely upside down. The experience with people changed my life. It broadened me beyond my family, beyond my community. So three experiences had a great influence on my commitment to work with the poor: (1) visiting the Catholic worker and meeting Dorothy Day; (2) reading Msgr. Ryan's pamphlet; and (3) meeting the people in Friendship House.

For many years I was able to keep up a relationship with Dorothy. I felt very good that soon after I was ordained in 1956, Dorothy called me. I went over to Staten Island to bless their new farm. Even that was an experience for me. I grew up with all the rigidity of the Catholic Church at that time, including very strict rules on the celebration of liturgy. At the blessing there were little kids with balloons yelling and screaming with goats and chickens all over the place. There was nothing formal about the place or the blessing. I had just come out of six years of very formal seminary training. Now I was experiencing another way of doing things, a much more human way.

Remember I said my first parish was not just middle class but the wealthiest parish in the Diocese of Brooklyn. I was in that parish for 7 years. I went there right after my ordination in 1956. The following year, 1957, the Diocese of Brooklyn was split. Where I was, St. Agnes in Rockville Centre, became the Cathedral Church of the newly formed Diocese of Rockville Centre and I became the Master of Ceremonies at the Cathedral (believe it or not).

During my seminary years, I had almost left to join Maryknoll to work in Latin America. I had become familiar with the problems of Latin America as president of the Seminary Mission Club. But I changed my mind and began to prepare myself to work with Puerto Ricans who were coming to areas of Brooklyn in great numbers. I never expected to become the Master of Ceremonies at the Cathedral Church in a new diocese. In 1958 I approached the new Bishop of Rockville Centre, Bishop Kellenberg, and I requested a leave of absence so I could go with Maryknoll to Latin America. His response to me was very clear: "not now or ever." So there I was.

By that time I was beginning to make contact with various people. There were Mexicans living above stores in Rockville Centre. I was able to use my Spanish with them. I also had contacts in the Black Community in Rockville Centre. I had started a Christian Family Movement (CFM) group which was very interesting. It began in 1957 with two couples. When I left in 1963 we had 42 couples. They were very involved with issues in Rockville Centre, such as housing and urban renewal. They are still close friends of mine. Remember this is 45 years ago.

So instead of going with Maryknoll to Latin America, I was assigned to The Catholic University in Washington, D.C. to study, and I eventually became the founding principal of Holy Trinity High School in Hicksville, Long Island where I remained for two years. They were good years and I enjoyed them but I knew in my heart that this work was not for me. In my first year at Holy Trinity we had 600 students. I knew every student by name. I could greet each one of them personally and by name in the hallways or in the classrooms. The next year we had 1200 students with a goal of 2,400 students over the next two years. I did not know 1200 students by name and I could see myself being the big king on his throne in an office without any contact with students, doing all sorts of administrative work. I knew it was not for me.

I wrote to Bishop Kellenberg and he was very good to me. He responded and told the personnel board that I had not requested the assignment to Holy Trinity High School, that I was a hard worker and the board should do what seemed best. I asked to go back to regular parish work or to have a special assignment in race relations. The board assigned me to Miraculous Medal in Wyandanch and in so doing filled both my requests. I was sent to Wyandanch as an assistant pastor. The parish was dead. There was nothing happening. It was "death warmed over." I inherited a "youth program" with two kids who were going only because their parents made them go. It was a challenge.

The community was, at that time, 96% Black, with two to three percent Hispanic. The Church community was predominately White with very few Blacks and Latinos coming to Church. We worked closely with the Black community on various social issues. It was a great experience for me. I learned a lot. I stayed in Wyandanch for 16 years. I was first an assistant pastor and then administrator. They offered the parish to five priests all of whom turned it down until one of them said, "Offer it to Andy. He is the only one who really wants it." So that was the way I became pastor of Miraculous Medal in Wyandanch in 1974. Soon after John McGann became Bishop of Rockville Centre, I thought about writing to him about going to Latin America. But I realized this was not the time. I had become the pastor of the poorest parish in the diocese. I said to myself, "Let me see what I can do here." So I stayed for 16 years.

By 1983 I was getting anxious. Even though I still saw many things that had to be done in Wyandanch, I realized I was not getting any younger. I was 53 years old. If I did not make a move at that time, I would never go to Latin America, which was still on my mind. I wrote to Bishop McGann and I met with him. I told him I wanted to resign as pastor, take a six-month sabbatical and go to Latin America with Maryknoll. My idea was to go to El Salvador where Archbishop Romero and others were dying for their faith. Bishop McGann was very generous. He gave me everything I asked for, except the place. In God's providence, I did not go to El Salvador but to the Dominican Republic.

Fr. Tom Maloney was working in the Rockville Centre Diocesan Mission at that time in the Dominican Republic. He knew I was interested in Latin America and asked me if I would join him in the Diocesan Mission. My response to him was, "No." Then I thought about it. I was, after all, a diocesan priest and I had some responsibilities to the diocese. The Bishop was thinking of closing down the mission because no priest was interested in going and the Bishop would not let Tom Maloney work alone. I told the diocese that I would take a look at the mission. I went to the Dominican Republic for a month. It was not as exciting as El Salvador but I could see there was a lot to do. So I went to the Dominican Republic and stayed in the parish of San Pedro Apostol in El Cercado for 17 years. They were good years. Even at the end when I was away a lot because of some surgery and other difficulties, I maintained the relationship of pastor.

By 1990 I was drinking too much. On some days I started drinking early in the morning and by noon time my speech would be slurred. I tried to stop drinking on my own but I was not successful. My life was out of control. Tom Mahoney and Sister Jane Riley tried to intervene on a few occasions. They confronted me about my excessive drinking. I finally realized they were right. I needed help. I could not control my drinking on my own. We informed Bishop McGann and he assigned me to Guest House, an AA-based program outside of Detroit. I stayed there for a full three months. I am a recovering alcoholic. I have not had a drink for 15 years. I am absolutely convinced that God intervened in my life to save me. An alcoholic focuses on self. A recovering alcoholic focuses on others. Christians should be the healthiest people of all because we are called to love one another. I quickly learned that AA is a spiritual program that calls for a conversion from love of self to love of others. I have written a little piece called "A Letter to God from an Alcoholic." I'd like it to be part of my interview.

All Catholic social teaching is based on the dignity of each human person as a child of God. Whatever increases a person's dignity is good. Whatever decreases that dignity is evil. I can look back on three things that I am proud of because they added to the dignity of the people in El Cercado. First, we built an outhouse for each family so people would not be embarrassed when they went to the bathroom. Secondly, we installed solar-operated pumps to bring clean water to all the villages in the mountains so women would not have to walk miles each day to bring back fresh water. Third, we built a school so no child would have to admit that she or he could not read.

I did not come back to the Diocese of Rockville Centre willingly. Bishop Murphy had to drag me back. I did not come back on my own. I came back because the Bishop ordered me back. I had no choice in the matter. When Bishop Murphy came to Rockville Centre I was up here recovering from surgery. He asked me what I wanted. I told him I wanted to return to the Dominican Republic. He preferred that I stay here and work with Latinos on Long Island. He did not have enough priests to care for them. Eventually, he let me go back to the Dominican Republic. Then in 2002 he called me back permanently to work in Rockville Centre. So here I am.

The Bishop assigned me to be the coordinator of Spanish ministry in the town of Brookhaven. There are eight parishes in Brookhaven with significant Spanish populations. It is my job to see that basic services are available for Latinos. What I am actually trying to do, since I was given no job description, is to organize the Spanish community so they are able to obtain services for their people. There are over 60,000 Latinos in Brookhaven and there are only two priests who speak Spanish. I am trying to develop lay leadership who will accept responsibility for their Church and for services from the town. I am trying to give Latinos a voice in their own affairs.

For me, if the priest is not immersed in his community, he is not doing his job. The word "priest" means "bridge." A priest is a bridge. If he is not anchored in both sides of the bridge, the bridge will collapse. So the priest must be anchored both in God and in his people. He has to know and be with his people. By definition the priest is to bring God to his people and his people to God. So he must be rooted in the life of his people. The image of the priest as a man "set apart" comes mostly from the celibacy requirement. Celibacy separates a priest from his people because he does not share their lives or their problems. Celibacy is, in many cases, a liability. It does not allow the priest to live the same life his people live. The priest must be part of the life of the community, not separated from it.

Having said that, let me be clear that celibacy has worked for me. I have often said: "I would not marry any woman who would be interested in me." At my age, I am, of course, accustomed to a celibate life. Also I think it is part of my nature to be celibate. It certainly frees me up to go to people and do things I could not do if I were married. No woman could have lived with me for the past 50 years. She would never have seen me. Even now, with the work I am doing, I am out almost every night of the week. We have a deacon who is over-involved in the life of the parish. He hardly ever sees his wife. He knows it. I do not have to spend time with a family because I do not have a family. My family is my people. I could, if I so desired, sit in this room and do nothing. But that does not interest me. I would not be functioning as a priest. For me, celibacy has helped my priesthood. On the other hand, marriage offers its own opportunities to a priest to minister in an entirely different way. The married priest can bring something to ministry that a celibate priest simply can not bring. Both have legitimacy. But for me, celibacy has worked well. For the Church, celibacy should be optional. I am amazed how much we talk about celibacy and how little we talk about poverty. Jesus, on the other hand talked a lot about simplicity of life and spoke very little about celibacy.

I do not consider myself poor. I have a computer and small but comfortable rooms. My basic needs are satisfied. Coming out of working in Wyandanch for 16 years and the Dominican Republic for 17 years, I have been deeply involved in the lives of super poor people. With this background I can not consider myself poor. On the other hand, I own nothing except a computer and a car. I do not have one penny in a savings account. I just do not own things. I think poverty has enhanced my personal life and my ministry. I do not worry about material things at all. I do not own property. If I am going to work with poor people, I do not see how I can be even moderately wealthy and be real with them. At times I feel guilty or I am embarrassed by the comfortable life I do lead when I know that the people I have been working with most of my life have zero, nothing at all. I have to keep in mind the words of St. Leo the Great, "His gain will be greatest who keeps the least for himself." Most of my money goes out right away. I send money to families in the Dominican Republic and I know I am keeping some families alive, people who without me have no other means of support. I am afraid they will lose this support when I retire next year and my salary goes way down. At the end of last month, I was afraid I would not have enough money for gas. I had $10 in my checking account and, as I said, I do not have a savings account. I got through it and I'm still here.

I do not own stocks because it would be buying into a system that produces so many poor people in the first place. By the way, it isn't just priestly poverty we should be talking about but poverty in the Church and poverty among the Christian people. Practically speaking, we rarely preach about poverty. People do not want to hear it. I am not talking about having necessities (and putting children through college can be considered a necessity). I'm talking about luxuries that people do not want to give up. Many people have a life style of luxury and become very upset if this is pointed out to them. But they shouldn't worry. Most bishops and priests have a luxurious life style and are not going to preach on poverty.

Besides chastity and poverty, prayer is important to me, more important than it used to be. In my drinking days, prayer had little importance for me. Being sober I look at life differently and prayer has taken on a much greater importance. My attitude towards prayer might be different than most people's attitude. The ideal of prayer came out of the monastic life style and it is not necessarily the ideal for busy people including the diocesan priest. Yet I find it important to take a few minutes every morning and every night to pray, not necessarily for long periods of time. For me, prayer is putting my life in conformity with Jesus and the Gospel. Prayer is a time of reflection when I make sure that in my work I am building the kingdom of God and not my own kingdom.

It all goes together. We must try to bring together the liturgy of the Church and the social teaching of the Church. This is where God's kingdom is found. A community that is seeking social justice must worship the God of justice. The community that is worshiping God must recognize that their God is a God of justice. A community can not worship adequately if the community is not involved in the work of social justice. The two are so intimately bound up that if we lose sight of one, we lose sight of the whole and we lose sight of the Kingdom of God.

I am not a prophet and so I will not even try to predict the future of the Church especially since I can not predict the working of the Holy Spirit in the Church. Also I do not have a lot of contact with young priests and I certainly would not put "all" young priests in a certain category. Having said that, it seems to me that the future of the Church is somewhat "blah." I do not see much interest in social justice issues on the part of young priests. A poor parish near Wyandanch had a hard time finding a pastor. No one volunteered. Finally a priest was assigned. So while we can not predict the future, the future does not look bright for the Diocese of Rockville Centre. We have inherited a hierarchy that resists change. We need to elect bishops and have optional celibacy for priests so there can be greater diversity among both bishops and priests. That's as far as I will go in predicting the "Church of the future." As I said, we can not predict the workings of the Holy Spirit.

Excerpts from "A Letter to God from an Alcoholic":

Slowly, about twenty some years ago, I began to find a new companion, a new God, if you will. I began to find comfort and relaxation in alcohol. He was a faithful friend; even though I had to buy his friendship, he was always there, very tangible, seemingly very real. Your friends saw what was happening and confronted me. With a boundless trust in you and a baseless trust in me, they spoke with your voice. I resisted but finally gave in. For three days I struggled with this until, by your gentle graces, I was able to say that I am an alcoholic, that I could not control my drinking. I needed help from others. I needed your help if I was ever going to be rescued from this slavery. This great god, Andrew, surrendered to his true God, You. My history gives me little hope that I will be faithful. Your history gives me every hope in the world that you will keep me faithful, if only I will let you. With your grace I will be fully aware that alcohol is my implacable enemy, and only in You will I find "this tremendous lover."

Sincerely,
Andrew P. Connolly

CHAPTER FOUR

REV. BRYAN J. KARVELIS

MISSION TO THE POOREST

I have been in one parish, Transfiguration in Williamsburg, Brooklyn, for 50 years. I think it has been a gift from God, a gift to me and hopefully a gift to others. I have grown enormously. My priesthood has become dearer and dearer to me with each passing year. Now in my "old age" I am very, very happy, extremely happy and extremely grateful. It has been a wonderful experience. I realize it might not be for everyone to be in the same parish for so long, but for me it has been a grace, an extraordinary gift.

I have always felt an attraction to people who are poor. I don't know why. It was always in me — even as a kid. I did not understand it. I am sure one reason I wanted to become a priest was that I could work with poor people. I don't know where it came from.

My family was the typical, second generation Irish-American family. During the depression, we had a hard time like so many families around us. We did not have a lot of things but we always had enough to eat. We had our own house. I was conscious that while we did not have a lot we had enough. But the biggest influence in my life came while I was in the major seminary.

At the end of my first year in the seminary, I told my spiritual director, Msgr. Coffey, that I was organizing a group of my classmates to study Aristotle's Ethics. He advised me not to do that. Rather, he said we should use our time to meet people. He wrote on a piece of paper the names of people he wanted me and my group to meet. The first name was Dorothy Day at the Catholic Worker. Then came the Baroness de Hueck at Friendship House and then Ed Wilox of *Integrity Magazine*. They were all wonderful people, but it was Dorothy who inspired me the most. Here I was, a young man who wanted to work with the poor and there was Dorothy doing it now. I remember walking into the Worker on the Bowery in lower Manhattan for the first time on a Friday around noon. Dorothy was serving pea soup to the people on a line. After she served the soup, Dorothy did not seem anxious to leave so we sat down and talked. I was profoundly impressed by her. I said to myself, "this is Church" even though I had never seen anything like it in the Church. I knew immediately this is what I wanted to do. I wanted to be like Dorothy Day. She was so obviously dedicated to the poor and so obviously committed to struggle with the poor. I started to read the *Catholic Worker* and *Commonweal* because Dorothy wrote for both publications. I tried to read everything she had ever written. Like her, I wanted to be involved in the work for justice for oppressed people. But I wondered how it could work out that I would be a priest in Brooklyn working with poor people.

Back in the seminary an older seminarian, John Lynch, knew of my interests and asked me to give a talk to the entire student body about the Puerto Rican immigration into Brooklyn. I told John that I could not give the talk until I had more contact with Puerto Ricans. So during the Christmas vacation I contacted Catholic Charities, which in turn put me in touch with a reporter from the old *Brooklyn Eagle* who had contact with some Puerto Rican families. He took me to meet them and strangely enough in the same parish where I would spend my entire time in the priesthood – Transfiguration parish.

I remember walking into a two-bedroom apartment with 11 people. I knew again, right away, that this was the ministry for me. I wanted to be with people I could help, live with, share with, bring them the Gospel and be with them in their struggle for justice. Certainly the injustices committed against them were enormous.

In those days the Puerto Ricans were the immigrants. They were discriminated against on the job, in their pay and working conditions. Fair labor laws did not apply to them. As soon as I was assigned to Transfiguration as a priest, I immediately began to organize demonstrations at local factories that employed Puerto Ricans. I soon came to realize that I could not help the people on a one-to-one basis. Even though one-to-one is important, like getting the people full welfare benefits and access to the hospitals, more needed to be done. I also had to look at the causes of poverty. Slowly, with God's grace, I was developing a commitment to live with the poor and join in their struggle against the causes of poverty.

We found out about the discrimination against immigrants. They were not paid a living wage, for example. They were put into sub-standard housing and charged high rents. I saw the need to help people one-by-one in direct services. But also I had to work with them to change the system that was oppressing them—unjust working conditions, for example. I had to do both things even though most of our training was in providing direct services.

It was all part of priesthood, all part of proclaiming the Good News of the Gospel. You can't tell a person to come to church and pray and return to an apartment in the winter without heat or hot water. You can't tell people to accept their poverty and their low wages and the abuse and the discrimination against them as if it were God's will for them. It is not God's will for them. God's will is their well being. No, as priest and leader you have to help your people have a better life. You have to tell people that God is love and show it by joining with them to fight for what they need to live a good human life. I never saw any of this as being anything but part of my priesthood. It is all part of proclaiming the Gospel that God is love. We have to say it and the people have to see it in us. Let me give you an example.

At the present time, there are about 30 male immigrants living in the rectory. The numbers fluctuate between 26 and 30. They are, for the most part, undocumented and homeless. I give them a place to live and I become more of a father and they become more of my family. Some have stayed for years, most for less time. There is a constant but slow turnover. Each year four or five men leave and others come to take their place. I charge rent: $30.00 per month, per person. That goes to pay the expenses of a large house: heat, lights, hot water, for example. The costs are enormous. The rent money does not include food. The men take care of their own food. They buy it and they cook it themselves.

We have a regular shelter for the homeless in addition to the rectory. We can basically take in off the streets anyone who has no place to stay. This is more temporary housing than the rectory. We encourage these men to see a social worker and get a job so they can get on their feet as soon as possible.

We have opened up a place for people with AIDS. There are 21 people living there. It used to be that we'd have a person dying each month, but now with new medications the mortality rate is much lower. We still have people dying but not nearly as frequently as we used to have.

Many years ago we opened up a Social Service Mission in which we see people who need direct services in such areas as disputes with landlords, problems with Medicaid, welfare or immigration. Anyone who has a problem can come and we try to straighten it out. In the beginning I was doing it myself but it quickly became too much for me. I had volunteers but that was not enough. Then in the late 60's Catholic Charities gave us a social worker. With the War on Poverty we began to get government funding and we still do but under this administration we get less and less each year. Government money funds the Mission but we are constantly being cut.

The Mission is a multi-service facility. We work with our people so that they receive proper medical treatment and see that it is covered by Medicaid or Medicare. We deal with housing problems and immigration services. We have two offices for immigrants, most of whom are undocumented. It used to be that the INS would conduct raids at factories and put the undocumented in jail. I remember going to prisons to get people out. Thank God those kinds of things have stopped. Now the services are more in the fields of legal help and counseling. Ann Pillsbury handles cases from Central America and Sr. Peggy Walsh handles everyone else. This program has also experienced cutbacks and we are not sure what will happen to the program over the next couple of years. We will try our best to continue. The need is great.

Another major issue in Williamsburg is housing Housing is always a major problem for poor people in Williamsburg. But it has become even more so recently with the "invasion" of yuppies and the Hasidic people. Yuppies are able to pay higher rents, so landlords are anxious to get rid of poor Hispanic people and charge the yuppies $2,000 to $3,000 a month rent. Gentrification has become a big problem and its effect on poor people is dreadful. Lofts have been turned into luxury apartments overlooking the East River with a great view of Manhattan. It may be that my ability to work with the poor in Williamsburg is at an end because soon there will be no more poor people left in Williamsburg. How ironic!

We have managed to unite most of the parishes in Williamsburg and Greenpoint with the parishes in Bedford-Stuyvesant being interested. This means we will have 27 or 28 parishes organized around housing issues and the city is starting to take notice. We are insisting that not all of the new housing be high-rise luxury apartments but that a certain number be set aside for the poor.

These things happen very quickly. Someone buys an abandoned factory. It is quickly turned into luxury apartments. Yuppies rent the apartments and there is no room for the poor. Other landlords see what is happening and begin to convert their apartments into luxury apartments, knowing that the yuppies will meet their price. So landlords renovate, get rid of the poor and rent to yuppies. It is a sad situation.

It is hard to talk to them. They do not appear to be organized. Now the Hasidim are doing the same thing but from a totally different viewpoint. They have very large families – 12 or 13 children per family. Their population is expanding rapidly. They obviously are trying to take over the neighborhood. I resist that and I've been called anti-Semitic.

The new Bishop of Brooklyn, Bishop DiMarzio, supports the efforts to organize the parishes but he is sensitive to the charge of anti-Semitism. Bishop Joe Sullivan has been working with us and from his long history in the diocese he knows what is going on. We are uniting with poor people and once again we are a part of their struggle for decent housing.

At a recent cluster meeting of priests, a religious order priest said he would not announce at Mass the date and time of a coming demonstration. He said he would not announce it in church because the church is spiritual and this demonstration was secular. I was shocked by his comments even though I had heard that this idea was common among young priests. For them, the church is spiritual; a demonstration for adequate housing is secular and, as such, had no place in the church. I wonder how anyone can preach the good-news to the people without trying to give them concrete good-news, like decent housing for their families.

I distinguish between the sacred and the secular. But if a priest works with people on justice issues such as fair housing, I do not see this as secular. It is helping your brother or sister in need. It is bringing good-news in a very real way. It is trying to live the Gospel "I was a stranger and you welcomed me."

We give direct service to hundreds and hundreds of people. Probably most of them do not come to Mass on Sunday. But they do know the Catholic Church helped them when they needed help and that is what Jesus was all about – helping people in need. It is hard to say what effect these memories have later on. But helping people in need is a very powerful way of proclaiming Gospel.

Jesus healed the sick. In those days, that was the best help a person could give. Today we have modern medicine that can do some won-

derful things, so we take healing more for granted, but not in the time
of Jesus. Our work in housing provides shelter for the homeless and
for those with AIDS. This is our way of doing what Jesus did. We can
not heal someone who has a broken leg, but we can get good medical
care for that person. Again, this is our way of doing what Jesus did and
when it is done with love by loving people, it is our way of healing in
the 21st century. It is our way of preaching the good news in our time
just as Jesus preached the good news in his time. He made himself
available to people and we try to make ourselves and our services available to people, no questions asked. If you need help and we can do it,
then we do it.

There is no doubt in my mind what it is that has sustained me
over these 50 years. It all started with growing up in a beautiful family
and it developed during the years in the seminary. But the most significant factor for me has been the spirituality of the Fraternity of
Charles de Foucauld, the Jesus Caritas Fraternity. Struggling to live a
life among the poor as modeled in the life of Brother Charles has
strengthened me enormously. I can't believe that I have found myself
in the same situation that Brother Charles would have chosen were he
alive today.

In the parish we now have 17 fraternities that meet independently
on a regular basis to develop their spirituality. They form the back-
bone of the parish and they are a support to me. I also belong to a
priest fraternity. I tried to form a religious order but it did not work
out. I wanted to call the order "The Little Brothers of the Word."
They would have been workers, full-time workers in a parish.

The Little Brothers of the Word would have been either priests or
brothers. The brothers would have done most of the manual labor.
One brother was with me for 30 years. He just died recently.

Applicants came, lived the life for a while but did not stay. I was no more successful than Brother Charles himself. God has given me the grace of these fraternities and they have been a great support for me in the parish.

So I have a rather unique relationship in the parish. I share my spiritual life with the members of the parish fraternities. Each fraternity has two weekend retreats each year. I am always there for these retreats but I don't attend the weekly meetings of each fraternity. It would be too much. I have chosen not to attend these weekly meeting because they have their own leaders called the "Responsible." I meet with all of the leaders on a monthly basis. This is the Parish Council. They tell me what the people are suffering from and what the problems are. We listen to each other, exchange and make plans to address the problems. It works well. They represent 400 people who are struggling to live the Christian life, obviously some more than others. They form a great spiritual support for me. I'm sure that it is because of them that I've been able to survive.

Another support that Brother Charles insisted upon was getting away each month for a "Day of Desert." I've been ironclad on this for myself. Every Thursday and Friday I get away from Transfiguration and go to our retreat house, Tabor, in Tarrytown. I'm usually alone although since I've been sick I've had someone with me. It gives me a chance to walk in the woods and renew myself. So I have a Day of Desert each month, a day of prayer each week and an hour of prayer each day. Without all this I'm not sure how I would have survived or even if I would have survived.

I take a month's vacation each year and I take it at Tabor. People are free to come up with their families. It is a very peaceful time, a time for prayer, a time for rest and a time to enjoy nature. God has given us this incredibly beautiful place for a retreat house for me and for the parish. We are surrounded by the Rockefeller's 5,000 acre estate which is all virgin forest. This is how I have survived and it helps a lot of our own people to survive.

I'm poor. I don't measure poverty in dollars and cents, although it has a lot to do with it. The poverty Brother Charles taught us is far more impressive: you don't have anything that would separate you from the poorest of the people you serve and among whom you live. So I moved out of the rectory and lived in a tenement for 16 years. Then I realized that the poorest of the people in the parish were living in the rectory so I had to come back. If I wanted to live among the poor, the best place for me was in the rectory with the undocumented men. But it is a very different kind of rectory. We have no cook, no cleaning lady, no servants. I'm living among the poorest. We all feel very comfortable. This is the kind of poverty I'm talking about. It is a poverty that does not emphasize whether or not you buy something or you don't buy something. I own a car, for example, a Chevy Cavalier. I need a car but I always buy a used one. Without a car I could not get away to Tabor for my days of desert and I'd go bananas. So a car is necessary for me. But the men in the rectory use it also. Someone put an air conditioner in my bedroom but I don't use it. If the other men do not have air conditioned bedrooms then neither will I. I could not sleep in luxury while they are sweating. The emphasis is being with the poor and living as the poor, being a little brother to them.

No question about it. If I dressed as a "Monsignor" with red buttons and a red sash, no one would come within 10 feet of me. It would be ridiculous. I'm so grateful the Diocese lets me stay here. I've been here for such a long time and I've given the rectory over to undocumented immigrants. It's working well here and the Diocese has left me alone. I remember when Bishop Mugavero came to see me in the apartment. When he left he said, "God bless you, Bryan. I could not live here for one day but I'm glad you're doing it." He was a very pastoral man, a real brother. Most of what I've been able to do is because of him and I'm very grateful to him.

I always used to tell the people that "I am Spanish by heart." When one of the men of the parish heard I was having kidney problems, he came forward, without being asked, and donated a kidney. We were compatible, so he gave me a kidney. When I came back to the parish from the hospital, I told the people, "I used to say I was Hispanic by heart. Now I can say I am Hispanic by flesh and blood also."

The surgery was a great success but the side effects have been terrible. I don't have one-tenth of the energy I had before the surgery. I've not been feeling well at all. God alone knows how much time I have left here on earth. Whatever it is, it's alright with me. I'm convinced the will of the Father for Jesus was to proclaim Gospel, the good-news, the Kingdom of God. Jesus proclaimed this Gospel in good times and bad times. He proclaimed Gospel when the people were listening and accepting his message. When he was put on trial, he continued to proclaim the good-news. He did it by dying. I want to imitate that as much as possible. I intend to keep preaching the good-news in good times and bad times. It is easy to preach the good-news when you are feeling well and you have plenty of energy. It is difficult when you are not feeling well. I hope to do as well as I can with the health I have left.

I am so grateful for my illness. It has taught me a great lesson about the kingdom of God. I had thought the Kingdom of God meant to spread God's kingdom of love by loving as God loves us and that is true. But there is another aspect to the kingdom which is just as important: receiving love in joy and gratitude. If you do not receive love in joy and gratitude you don't give it either. At this stage of my life I find myself receiving from many, many, many people. At the beginning of my illness I wanted to be independent. Then I realized: wait a minute. This is all part of the Kingdom of God. I'm their little brother. They consider themselves brothers and sisters to me. I'm so grateful and humbled for all these experiences of God's Kingdom.

As long as God wants me to stay, I will stay. But if I should die tomorrow, the parish and the work of the parish would continue provided the priest who comes to take my place will allow what is here to continue. If the diocese will leave it alone, it will survive.

We must look within the parish itself and tap the leadership that is already here. They are trained and willing and able to take over. During the last two years I've been in and out of hospitals and away from the parish more than I've been in it. I was so happy to see how smoothly the programs in the parish ran without me. No problem. I'm sure it would be the same if I should die tomorrow. Of course, what might end the parish is the Yuppie invasion. We'll have to see. But if our people are not pushed out and continue to remain here, the parish will continue to survive and flourish.

I am happy that the people see me as celibate and the sisters as celibate. They have also seen a number of priests who have married and continue to live and work in the parish. The people love them as much as they love me. I am very pleased with this. In the beginning there was some tension regarding John Mulhern and Luz. But when the people saw how good they were and saw other priests married and working in the parish, all were accepted. We presently have three married priests, all bilingual, who live within walking distance of the Church.

But they could do more. They could celebrate the Eucharist, for example, if we had permission. It does not make any sense that I have to celebrate three or four Masses on a Sunday and two every day. It would be far better for the people to go to Mass celebrated by various priests and to hear different homilies, instead of listening to me all the time.

John Mulhern is a tremendous help to me. He knows the parish inside out. He volunteers three days a week to direct the Mission and all that goes on there. I talk to him the same way we talked when he was an active, celibate priest here. The two other married priests are also deeply involved. One heads up "Casa Bethsaida" the home for people with AIDS, a very challenging job and he does it well. All three are very good men and they are a great help to me. As I said, I wish they had permission to do more.

I'd just like to return to the Fraternity of Charles de Foucauld before we finish up. The goal of the fraternity is that we become truly contemplative, while living not in a monastery but in the world, or in my case, in a parish. That was Brother Charles' intuition, his grace. I see action and contemplation as being complementary to each other, not opposed to each other or separated from each other. I've seen it in my own life how one depends so deeply on the other. If I did not have hours of contemplative prayer each day, after a while I'd have nothing to say to the people.

I spend about two hours in contemplative prayer each day and it is up to me to find the time to do this. Then there is my weekly "Day of Desert" at Tabor. I am not saying this is always pleasant time. The Dark Night of the Soul can be very unpleasant. But I know that God is present to me even when I do not feel God's presence. The time given to prayer has had a great impact on me and on what I think and say and do. I am absolutely sure of this. And this spirit of prayer is growing in the parish. For example, before evening Mass in the chapel, there will be 30 to 40 people spending a half hour in prayer before the Blessed Sacrament. Most will be members of one of the parish's Charles de Foucauld Fraternities. They are coming home from work in a factory and come to the chapel for private prayer and the Eucharist.

I could not imagine myself in any other way except living with the poor for the sake of Jesus and the Gospel. I need the poor more than they need me. They need help but so do we. It is in helping them that I realize how much I too am in need. Some times they can drain you and you have to know when to let go. But they are always very gentle and supportive. I could never say I'm lonesome. I receive so much love and concern from the people. I am not sure I would get the same kind of love and concern from other people as I get from poor people.

Certainly it is encouraging for me to see how many good and simple people, who do not have many of this world's possessions, have embraced the Gospel. I do not want to compare them to other groups of people but I do know that many poor people are deeply committed to Jesus and the Gospel. They depend on God because they do not have material goods to depend on. Maybe that is what Jesus meant when he said,

"BLESSED ARE THE POOR"

Bryan Karvelis died on October 18, 2005.

Writing for *The New York Times* after the funeral Mass on October 23, 2005, Manny Fernandez wrote: It was clear yesterday that it was not the pastor's longevity that people came to remember. It was something more. Monsignor Karvelis' absence, like his presence, would be immense. People found it easier to talk about the past rather than the future. Some people said he had made them strong in their Catholic Faith. Some said he had inspired them to work with the poor, to pray more often. Others simply said the church would never be the same.

He lived simply, humbly, but acted boldly, extravagantly.

CHAPTER FIVE

REV. JOSEPH D. DIELE

CAN THE CHURCH BE REFORMED FROM WITHIN?

I was ordained May 18, 1985.

I had been most inspired by the inner city priests that I knew, so I asked the Assignment Board to assign me to Our Lady of the Presentation in Brownsville, as my first parish. I was there for three years with John Powis. Then I spent the next three years at Kings County Hospital, as chaplain. I always had the desire to do hospital work. The opening came and John was getting ready to leave Presentation so it looked like the right move for me.

I did a lot of counseling, a lot of work with the families of the patients. I was a part-time social worker and part-time priest. It was a real good experience for me and taught me a great deal, but I wanted to get back to parish work.

I heard that St. Ann's was open and nobody wanted to go there. Fursey O'Toole had been there as pastor for 10 years and was being assigned to St. Patrick's. The parishes of St. Michael – St. Edward and St. Ann – St. George had been grouped as one parish.

I called Bishop Daily on his private number that he had given to all the priests and told him I'd like to go to St. Ann's. He gave me an immediate appointment. I shared with him some of my ideas. He seemed to listen. I got a call later that since I was the "best qualified," which meant that since I was the "only applicant," I was being assigned to St. Ann's. St. Ann's turned out to be a wonderful, wonderful experience for me.

Daily felt at that point there was no evangelization going on in St. Ann's and he was thinking of closing it. I had a simple idea: just go through the projects as frequently as possible and meet the people. We put up signs in front of the Church, which was officially St. George - St. Ann's since St. Ann's Church as such was already closed and I would live in St. George and use St. George as the Church. (Remember they were only a block apart.) We wanted to tell people that we were open and they were welcome.

I made it clear to the bishop that if I were to bring the people of the neighborhood to church, then the old Lithuanian former pastor who celebrated a Mass each Sunday in Lithuanian for a handful of people had to be taken care of somewhere else. St. George was no longer a Lithuanian parish but a parish for the Black and Latino peo-

ple of the neighborhood. The bishop agreed. He was also very supportive. He came every single month for two years to walk with me
through the projects — the 22 stories of the Faragut Housing Project.

He would come over after Mass at St. James Pro-Cathedral and
would spend two hours on a Sunday afternoon ringing doorbells with
me. He spoke Spanish, as you know.

I felt very much supported by Bishop Daily in the work of evangelization.

By "evangelization" I mean going out, meeting people, knocking
on doors, inviting people to Mass or other prayer services, Bible study
or other forms of religious instruction for adults and children.

There is another part of "evangelization." What are the needs of
the people? A big need for us in St. Ann's was security in the housing
projects. Women were getting raped or mugged when they went to the
basement to do their laundry.

We started "Mother Ann's Laundry Service" in the basement of
the Church. It was a contact with people that we never would have
had if we were not aware of the concrete needs of the people and if, as
a result, we had not started the "laundry business." We designated an
area in the basement of the Church and hooked up six washers and six
dryers.

It even produced a few jobs as we hired a couple of people to
wash, dry, and fold laundry for people who did not have time to do it
themselves. We provided the service while the one who dropped off
the laundry went out to do other things. We always inserted into the
laundry a prayer or a scripture reading.

It was "gentle evangelization." We also had a very active food pantry. In fact, it was often described as the largest food pantry in all of Brooklyn. It both answered a need and gave us more contact with people.

We did not ask questions. If a person came to the pantry, the person received food, no questions asked, much as Dorothy Day did. We made no distinctions between "deserving poor" and "undeserving poor." If you came to the pantry you "deserved" food.

We did all kinds of "youth stuff." Young people were made to feel welcome. We used a Montessori method of religious instruction from kindergarten to high school. It is called the "Catechesis of the Good Shepherd." It is fabulous. We had a pastoral associate, a lay person, with a Masters in Divinity from Union Theological. He and his wife started the program and supervised it.

She was a lawyer. They were both wonderful, wonderful people. He thought he had a vocation to the priesthood. But the whole celibacy thing got in the way. He was a spectacular pastoral associate. So we were able to do a lot of work with young people. The basement of St. Ann's became a safe haven for teenagers.

I would say that almost all the people who went through the RCIA were converts. Remember, we are dealing with small groups of people. We rarely, if ever, had more than 100 people at Mass on Sunday. But of the 100 people, more than 60 would be under the age of 20.

I did a thing that was unique. I lived there with a lay community. It was for me another way to live priestly life. The bishop was ok with it. There were six to nine of us, all men, living in the rectory. One was a Little Brother of Jesus.

We lived together and prayed together and we invited people in the neighborhood to pray with us. So when we said morning or evening prayers we would open the Church so people could join us and they did.

One was a man who lived in the housing projects. He was 67 years old when I first met him. He was into drugs and prostitution. That's how he made his money to live. He was an unlikely candidate, but there was something about him that I liked. I told him that if he joined us he'd have to give up his "business."

He thought about it for a few months and then came over to the rectory to say that he thought he was ready. I told him to keep his apartment for six months in case things do not work out.

He lived with me the whole time I was in St. Ann's. He was never on salary, of course, but he did all sorts of little things for us. He gave up drugs and alcohol and even stopped smoking. Of course, no more prostitution.

Some stayed longer than others. One fellow, John, thought of starting a religious order but things did not work out. Eventually, he became a Graymoor Friar. Dennis lived with us for about five years. We all ate together and took turns preparing the meals. On the nights there was choir practice we encouraged people to come early and have supper with us. Same with the nights when we had Bible Study.

Rarely did we have less than 20 people for dinner. It was a wonderful time.

We tried to be part of East Brooklyn Congregations (EBC) but we were kind of far away. We did some community organizing around the issue of a garbage dump in the Navy Yard which, as you know, is right next door to the Projects. We organized and we won. They removed the dump.

We also organized around the issue of bus routes and we got them to change the routes so that our people did not have so far to walk. It was an attempt to deal with the real issues as the people saw them. It was the other part of "evangelization" that I had spoken about before.

When I left St. Ann's, no full-time priest took my place. It was sad for me. I knew when I left that no one would ask to go there and no one would be assigned. I knew the whole thing would fall apart and it did.

I took a two-month vacation. When I came back they assigned me to St. Clare's in Rosedale. It turned out to be the worst four months of my life, a horrible time for me.

I felt bad about leaving St. Ann's. St. Clare's was not the kind of parish I wanted to be in. The pastor and I disagreed on everything. I felt that he was constantly yelling at me. I couldn't do this and I shouldn't do that. It was torture.

I went to the personnel board and asked for a transfer. They advised me to take some more time off, so I went on a six-month sabbatical. When I came back I was assigned to St. Patrick's – St. Lucy's as the assistant to Frank Shannon. They were the happiest six weeks of my life.

A priest had died there and they did not want to leave Frank alone, even though that would eventually happen. But it was such a wonderful time for me. Frank was the opposite of the former pastor. He was easy to get along with. As pastor he had to worry about money and administration. I was free to do the fun stuff, pastoral work.

There was a sister on staff also so we worked as a pastoral team together. It was healing for me after the four months in St. Clare's.

I am alone in St. Clement's in the sense that I am the only priest assigned to the parish. But I have a parish staff: a secretary who takes care of all the finances of the parish; two sisters, both are part time.

Both are SSND's. Sister Jean works on pastoral care with an emphasis on our aging population and spirituality. She is a spiritual director, gives retreats etc. She keeps us focused on the spiritual. Sister Pat works one-quarter time and is in charge of religious instruction. With her we have gone from 30 kids in the program to 60 kids and this within just a few months.

We are 100% Black with a few Latinos just starting to move into the outer fringes of the parish. I had a Baptism at Mass the other day and I did it all in Spanish. Not one person in the family spoke English.

We might, over time, become a bilingual parish and this will upset some people. It is a challenge we may face some day.

We had a school. It just closed. The children were spectacular and I loved going into the classes but it was such a drain on parish resources. We had a recent history of poor leadership and things went downhill quickly.

The New York City Board of Education is interested in the building. At first they said it would be an Early Childhood Center. Now they are talking about a school for 9th graders only. This is ok but I'll have to find out what some of the neighbors think. We'll have to see. I prefer an Early Childhood program.

We also have a convent. Catholic Charities had been in the building for many years but they pulled out. The SSND's were looking for a place, both as a residence and as an Educational Center for women. So we did it.

They came last year. Three sisters live here and four come in to run the Education Center for women. They give courses ranging from English as a Second Language to High School Equivalency. It is great. They also sponsor days of prayer and other programs for the women of the parish. They train women to be leaders. It has been a good relationship. All CCD classes are held in the Center. It has worked out well.

As a youngster growing up, I was influenced by St. Francis. Also, I remember my 7th grade teacher talking about Dorothy Day, Martin Luther King, Gandhi, people like that.

While I was in the seminary events took place that had an influence on me. I am referring to events like the assassination of Archbishop Romero and the killing of the four women in El Salvador. These events influenced me tremendously. People who were willing to die for the poor spoke to me.

Then meeting people like Bryan Karvelis and John Powis influenced me some more. Like them, I am a member of the Fraternity of Charles de Foucauld. These have been the influences in my life.

Unlike most priests I have a lot of contact with seminarians and younger priests. At St. Ann's I had enough money each year to pay a seminarian to work in the parish instead of working on Wall Street. I wanted to expose them to the kind of work that goes on in the inner city.

I have also tried to expand the Fraternities of Brother Charles and five seminarians are now in these Fraternities. This gives me contacts with them and gives me a chance to form, or at least influence, them.

I believe there are young priests and seminarians who are filled with zeal and who want to minister to the poor. However, they have fears. They are concerned about the Church and their role as priests. They wonder what they are getting themselves into.

There is a real love for the poor, but a love tempered with the realization that they don't know what their ministry will be like.

Every class is different. There are always those who have no desire to work with the poor. This has been true for a long time.

I don't have enough money at St. Clement's to hire a seminarian to work with me during the summer. We do have one seminarian who comes here every two weeks. He does some youth work and some outreach. That's my only connection right now. I still think it is worth the effort to expose seminarians to inner-city ministry.

I see myself as one of the baptized with the role of teaching and preaching but very much one of the baptized. Let me give you an example.

When I send out a letter to the people of the parish I sign it "Joe, your brother." I do not want "brother" capitalized. It is not a word of power. I am a human person struggling to be a good Christian.

Priesthood comes out of my baptism. My priesthood defines one of the ways to be a Christian, not the only way but certainly one of the ways.

To describe how I see my priesthood, I'd like to use the words of Joseph Campbell and the whole idea of being a myth maker.

My role is to take the mythology of Scripture and the mythology of worship and to use those stories to find meaning in life. In a more churchy way, my role is to be a minister of the word of God, to break open the stories, the myths, contained in Scripture and find meaning for people.

I try to show people that the stories of Scripture and the stories of the Sacraments are their stories not some one else's stories. A lot of younger priests feel more comfortable in the cultic role because their job description is clearer. I am not always sure what the hell I am doing except that I am meeting a need that has to be met, so I do it.

It is not enough that we tell the story of Jesus breaking the bread at the Eucharist, but we must be ready to break our bodies as Jesus did by being present here with one another. Jesus did more than break bread. He also died on the cross for us.

We must be daring enough to break ourselves in love for each other. It is what each of us is called to do, otherwise the Eucharist is just a story in the past without meaning for us.

We must read the story and live the meaning of the story. There is a reality in the Jesus story for us today. It is not enough for us to imitate at Mass what Jesus did but we are challenged by our baptism to do what Jesus did. We are called to be broken in love for one another.

I try to expose young priests and seminarians to these ideas. I consider my contacts with seminarians to be important. We pray together and go on retreats together and share together.

If priests, lay people and seminarians can feel comfortable by being themselves then there is no reason to create artificial barriers between clergy and laity. These barriers are the foundations of what is called "clericalism."

I'm talking about a group of lay people from different parishes who are trying to live in the spirit of the Fraternities of Brother Charles de Foucauld. We have joined together and we call ourselves the Nazareth Community.

The group is comprised of men and women. Some of the men are seminarians. There is now a married couple in the group. Our purpose is to pray together and share and grow together. I now have access to a house in Brooklyn. The Nazareth Community and other intentional communities meet there periodically.

It attracts people who want to deepen their spiritual lives and share on the level of faith. It fits very well into the purpose of all that we do in the parish; namely to connect us to God. My challenge to these communities is to spend not less than 2 hours a day in prayer.

I'm not saying it is easy. I'm saying it is important.

Sometimes I feel that I have accomplished nothing. But I also realize that over these 20 years I have walked with many wonderful people and I have allowed them to touch me, to change me, to challenge me, to show me something of God and to teach me how to be a human person. And for me to be a full human person, I need a relationship with God.

Yes, I realize that I have set up a certain number of programs, the pantry at St. Ann's for example. They have a life of their own but they are all temporal. They do not last. The relationships are the important things. They mean the most to me. I don't know about my effect on people but I am sure of their effect on me.

I think poverty has to be at the center of priestly life. But it is more than saying "I want to live in a poor parish and minister to the poor."

First of all, I have to see my own poverty. Then I have to recognize that I need God. Thirdly, I have to see what I am attached to, what I think I need. Poverty involves recognizing what I think I can not live without. It can be a thing or a person. Very often the clerical attitude is that because I am celibate I need a lot of toys. So a lot of priests, in good conscience, have toys. We need a greater emphasis on Christian poverty of spirit. Poverty has nothing to do with being a priest or not being a priest. It has to do with being a Christian. That's what we don't like to talk about.

We try to limit poverty to this or that group, the Catholic Worker, for example. It is the Christian vocation to not be so attached to a thing or a person that it hinders our relationship with God or with others.

While I consider myself poor, I do have a house that I use as a retreat house. I have always wanted a retreat house in the city. Why do we have to go away for a retreat?

Just about a year ago my grandmother's house, which is next to my mother's house in Brooklyn, became available. It was becoming too much for my mother to take care of and she did not want to sell it. I didn't have enough money to buy it, but I rent it from my mother.

I don't own it, so it fits into my simplicity of life style. The only thing I own is a car. But it allows me to have retreats within the city and to use it as a place where I can go on my day off to relax and pray.

If God is supposed to be at the center of our lives, then we must get rid of whatever clouds our vision of God. We can not let the vow of poverty become a vow of comfort.

People who are poor have to make choices. Many people with the vow of poverty have everything. As a Church we have not done well with this spirit of poverty thing that Jesus so often talked about.

I'd like to make a couple of reflections about celibacy. First of all celibacy is over-emphasized in our Latin Rite. It should never be mandatory. It has to be optional. For certainly, people who are not celibate are called to serve the Church and to serve the poor.

Celibacy should be an individual, personal decision, never an institutional decision. I am not minimizing how difficult it would be for a married priest and his wife to raise children in the housing projects. But that is their decision. If that is what they choose, God bless them. Amen.

Phil Berrigan and his wife did it. Look at the number of lay missionaries and their families who go to Third World countries. Their children are probably no more mixed up than any other children. We are making celibacy more important than the Sacraments. That is a mistake and it shows a wrong understanding of human sexuality.

When we pray for vocations we try to limit God to call only male celibates within a certain age range. It doesn't work and because it doesn't work people are deprived of the Eucharist.

There are plenty of people called to ministry and service and a few are male celibates. Business people use the book, *Who Moved My*

Cheese? If you keep going back to the same place to find the cheese and it is not there, you'd better look in some other places or else you'll starve.

The application to vocations is obvious. We'd better start looking for vocations in other places than male celibates or else we will starve and the people will starve for lack of Eucharist.

As pastor of a parish I lead a busy life and for me prayer is my source of energy. Sometime in college I developed a spirituality based on the spirituality of Charles de Foucauld which called for four hours of prayer/study each day.

I know that sounds like a lot, but I break up the four hours. I use time in the mornings and evenings and sometimes in the late afternoons between 4 and 5 p.m. I have a prayer room upstairs and I spend a good deal of time in the prayer room.

I meditate, read, study the scriptures and reflect on the readings for the coming Sunday. When things finally quiet down around here, I take about an hour to read the psalms, reflect on the day and pray for those who are sick or in trouble. So four hours of prayer includes spiritual reading, Bible study, sermon preparation as well as meditation.

I read commentaries on Scripture as well as traditional spiritual reading. At daily Mass I use some of the "Lectio Divina" techniques with the people for the homily. It is like the old "dialogue homily" with me summarizing the discussion.

On Sundays my homilies are long, about 35 to 40 minutes. Believe it or not, most of the people come back Sunday after Sunday.

It is kind of the Baptist style with an African twist to it. I keep learning. I try to keep observing the culture around me and to find the needs of the people rather than my own needs.

What has sustained me most over these 20 years are my friends. The friendships that I have are deep and important to me. My friends are women as well as men. Most of my classmates have left the active ministry. The people who sustain me are all lay people, although my closest friend happens to be a religious woman.

I've been a member of a priest Fraternity of Charles de Foucauld for about 18 years with the same group of priests. These relationships have sustained me. Also reading is important to me. I read a great deal, about 50 books a year, all kinds, novels, whatever I can get my hands on. These are all sources of renewal, but as I said, my lay friends are my greatest source of renewal.

Note: As of December 25, 2005, Joe Diele took a leave from active ministry of the Diocese of Brooklyn. He has become a full member as a priest in the Catholic Apostolic Church in North America (CACINA). He is putting together a parish community called The Church for All People.

He has been ex-communicated by the Catholic Bishop of Brooklyn, Bishop DiMarzio.

The journey continues. I have left CACINA. I informed them about a week ago. They are too similar to the Roman Church, too hierarchical, no sense that the people are the church, that it all starts with the people. I've been there, done that.

I do believe there is an advantage to being part of a larger federation or association, particularly if you need numbers for a demonstration against the war. So I will continue to look into that. When I announced to the congregation that I was leaving CACINA, I could tell by their reaction that it was irrelevant. It made no difference to them. What is relevant is that the Word of God be preached, that the sacraments be celebrated, that the Eucharist be offered, that we welcome the stranger and love one another. So for the present we do not belong to any diocese or federation, but we are OK.

When I wrote to the bishop, I listed eleven reasons why I felt I could not remain in the Catholic Church. These reasons include:

- "The place of women in the church."

- "The prohibition against divorced and remarried people receiving the Eucharist."

- "The treatment of gay and lesbian people as being intrinsically disordered and whose acts of affection are evil."

- "The horrible things said about women who have had to make the hard choice to have an abortion."

- "Mandatory celibacy for priests most of whom chose ministry and not celibacy."

- "Lack of collegiality even though it was so highly favored at Vatican II."

- "Too many regulations and laws at liturgy while prayer and the poetry of prayer are being intellectualized away."

- The priesthood has been reduced to a role of power over people. What happened to "I have come to serve, not to be served?"

- "Pastoring has been reduced to being a landlord. What happened to laying down one's life for the sheep?"

- "Those who have been abused are still in the background and not being cared for by the very church that has abused them."

- "Spirituality is only for the experts, not for lay people, the baptized."

When Bishop DiMarzio called the priests of the diocese to come together for a day of prayer and study on the topic of Evangelization, I went. When he announced that the secret resource of the Catholic Church in the work of Evangelization was its money, I said, "I'm out of here." I've written to the bishop giving him my 11 reasons for leaving. I asked for a meeting with him to discuss these issues.

My leaving has been joyful and peaceful. I'm working part time at Hospice. My mother has given me the use of this house that has been in our family for years. I preach and celebrate the Eucharist here. I counsel people here. We go on retreats. We have Bible study class. The congregation is small, about 50 people but very dedicated people. We are like a "house church" and we are happy about being small. Two young women have indicated that they feel called to the priesthood so they may serve the needs of the community as priests. We are looking into that. They need more Theology. When the time comes, they will be ordained by me and the people, the Church. We will ordain only as many priests as the community needs.

I'm busy and trying to be prayerful. People keep asking if I am married. The answer is "No" but I would be open to a relationship if it developed.

I was in a Charles de Foucauld priest support group for 20 years. Now that I've left the Catholic Church, I'm no longer welcome, even though I'm the same person I've been over these 20 years. I think they are afraid to be associated with me; the bishop might not like it. I am also not allowed to be on church property. Silly stuff!

At Mass I use various Eucharistic prayers, sometimes the Roman, but at other times the Lutheran or Episcopal. They are all beautiful and very similar. We have a good thing going on here.

I'll have to see where the Lord leads me and this movement.

CHAPTER SIX

REV. JOHN GILDEA

TEACHER OF THE WORD, MINISTER, AND LEADER

I was born and raised in Brooklyn, a member of Holy Name parish. I went to grammar school there. I had the Sisters of St. Joseph in the early grades and the Xaverian Brothers in the upper grades. I had a twin sister in the girls department, so I always knew what was going on or at least I thought I knew. It was a huge school.

I lived in a completely Irish community. Even though both of my parents were the only ones from their families who "came over," I still lived in a completely Irish community with plenty of aunts and uncles and cousins on the "other side."

The parish had a great influence on me and my brother and two sisters.

We had a lot of contact with the brothers. They ran the sports program. They trained the altar boys. Brother Donald and Brother Augustine had a great influence on me and on many other boys. Sister Helen had a great influence on the girls, not just with school subjects but with helping out on school activities like school dances. Things like that.

We had many vocations from the parish. One little statistic I like to quote to people is that in the 20 years from 1966 to 1986 there were 11 men ordained to the priesthood from Holy Name. Now there are not 11 men in the whole seminary. Each year there was also a constant flow of young boys and girls becoming Xaverian Brothers and Josephite Sisters. My twin sister is a Josephite. Through school and sports and personal contacts, the parish had a great influence on me and on many other young people at that time.

I went to Catholic high school in Manhattan, Power Memorial, run by the Irish Christian Brothers. Many of my friends from Holy Name went to Power Memorial High School and it certainly had an influence on me.

I was ordained for the Diocese of Brooklyn in 1966. My first assignment was to go to Puerto Rico to study Spanish at the Spanish Institute in Ponce, Puerto Rico, for about four months. John Powis was one of the priests who influenced me to volunteer for the Spanish Apostolate. I worked in his parish during the summers when I was in the Seminary. I got to know him pretty well. When I returned from Puerto Rico I was assigned to St. Matthew's on Eastern Parkway in Crown Heights. I lived in the rectory with four other priests. It was a pretty full house. We worked in the parish and covered four hospitals. Now there is only the pastor and a priest from Haiti. The hospitals are still there. It is still a good-sized parish, but the number of priests has gone from five to two. That is significant.

In 1968 the Diocese opened a mission in Paraguay, South America. I volunteered to go and much to my surprise I was selected, even though my Spanish was still poor and I was ordained for only two years. I knew the diocese wanted priests ordained for a minimum of at least three years. I spent the next five years on the missions. It was a great experience for me. Here I was living in the midst of an entirely different culture, a simpler, less materialistic culture. My Spanish improved a great deal. I've celebrated Mass more frequently in Spanish than in English.

When I returned from Paraguay I was assigned to my home parish, Holy Name. I was there for five years. My mother was still alive and living there. My father had died. Many of my classmates from grammar school were living there. By this time a large Spanish community had developed in Holy Name and they were my primary concern. I was the "Spanish priest." Then I volunteered for another "tour of duty" in Paraguay and I stayed there for three years. I was with Gene Connolly who stayed there for 30 years. The name of the parish was San Pedro in the Diocese of Coranova Piedo. I never met Father Tom Daily who was with the St. James Society in Peru. He would eventually become Bishop Daily, the Bishop of Brooklyn.

When Daily came to Brooklyn, he was interested in reviving the missionary effort of the Diocese since the mission in Paraguay had closed for a lack of volunteers. We suggested to him that he might look into the Dominican Republic, which he did. It was closer to home and a one-language country with a lot of Dominicans living in

Brooklyn. Daily went down to investigate and met Bishop Camilo and they decided to work together to set up a mission of the Diocese of Brooklyn in the Dominican Republic. I was on the committee to look for volunteers. We had only one, so I decided to apply. My mother had died so there was nothing to hold me back. Rockville Centre had also opened up a mission in the Dominican Republic but the two missions were not close to each other, about four or five hours apart by car.

I stayed in the Dominican Republic for four years. For most of that time I was alone. Some priests came down but none of them stayed. I contacted the bishop. I told him that I did not want to be alone any more. He agreed that to be alone was not a good thing for me. He did not want me to be alone. Also, I told him that I was not feeling well. I detected a lack of energy and I did not know why. Of course I was not getting any younger. The year was 1998. The next year I was diagnosed with cancer. It might have started when I was in the Dominican Republic. I was not interested in taking on all the responsibilities of being a pastor. The Diocese treated me well. I was sent to Our Lady of Fatima parish near La Guardia Airport. Ed Breen was the pastor. It was a nice assignment and I was very happy as the assistant pastor. My health had improved a bit.

The Diocese called me two years later and asked if I would be willing to put my name in to be the pastor of Sacred Heart parish down by the Navy Yard. I agreed but I let them know I would not be disappointed if I wasn't chosen. It wasn't the case that I had been at Our Lady of Fatima for two years and I was ready to become a pastor again. I don't think they got many applicants and I was chosen. You know, come to think about it, I might have been the only one who applied. I've been here for five years. When I arrived, Pedro Ossa was the pastor so it was Pedro and I, and he was here only for the next six or seven months. Sister Eileen, who has been here for 30 years, has been a great help. She knows the history of the parish and the people. She really functions as a pastoral assistant in the parish.

In the five years that I've been here I've also been the Administrator of Queen of All Saints for six months and administrator of St Michael – St. Edward's for the past year. So I'm the pastor here and the administrator of St. Michael – St. Edward's. My main responsibility is to serve the people in Sacred Heart and St. Michael – St. Edward's. I serve all of the people in the Fort Green Projects as well as the families on the side streets. Many Spanish families, Catholic, for the most part, are moving away and are being replaced by Black families, Protestant, for the most part. This has had an effect on Sacred Heart and St. Michael – St Edward's in the sense that fewer and fewer people are going to Mass. It is not a "doable" situation. Let me give you two examples.

Between these two parishes there are six parish buildings — all over 100 years old. The "newer" buildings were built in the 1890's. We are talking about churches, schools, rectories and convents. What bothers me is that I do not have the money to make the necessary repairs to keep all the buildings in good shape, so what's broken stays broken. People keep asking me to fix this or that but I don't have the money. This frustrates me. Also, I'm forced to spend a lot of time on maintenance of old buildings and I don't want to spend a lot of time doing that.

For me, stress comes on a Sunday when I don't have help and therefore I have to say three Masses. I have the 9 o'clock Mass here. Then I have to run to St. Michael's for the 10:15 and then back again to Sacred Heart for the 11:00. I feel guilty that I don't have enough time to talk to the parishioners who come to Mass and want to talk to a priest. I don't want to give the impression that I'm running away from people. I want to be a good pastor.

I've tried to make things work between the two parishes. We have a parish council to represent both parishes. We meet here and we have 8 people from Sacred Heart and 4 people from St. Michael – St. Edward's. I thought that was a fair way to represent both parishes in one council. On Christmas day we had only one Mass. It was bilingual at 10:00 am. I urged the people at St. Michael's to come and about 10 people showed up. I was gratified.

I think we are heading in the direction of having one parish with two worshiping sites. More and more children from St. Michael – St. Edward's are coming here for religious instruction. All baptisms and funerals are celebrated here. All parish records are now kept here. Sunday Masses are offered in both places.

Having said all this, I must now tell you that I'm being transferred to St. Martin of Tours in Bushwick. I will probably be leaving Sacred Heart in a month. St. Martin's is a big parish but I will not be alone. Bill Smith is already there. In fact I am not going as pastor. For the first six months I'll be the assistant pastor. They told me that they would like me to remain as pastor but if the work is too strenuous for me, they will move me to a smaller parish. Bill Smith will also move on and will be given a parish. They promised me that if I stay at St. Martin's, I will not be alone. All I know is that St. Martin's covers a very wide area. It is larger than my assignment at Sacred Heart. If I stay as pastor, they promised me an assistant. We'll see.

The official name for the parish is Martin of Tours – Our Lady of Lourdes. These two parishes have already been merged into one parish, although some of the canonical work still has to be completed. These two parishes contain eight buildings. I've gone from six buildings to eight buildings. The good thing is that these buildings are newer, not quite as old as the buildings in Sacred Heart and St.

Michael – St. Edward's. They appear to be in better shape, but I don't know for sure. I hope they are.

It does sound that again I'm not in a "doable" situation and if I go to St. Martin's, I'll be taking on more work, not less. I'll still be the pastor of two parishes. In fact I'll be the pastor of three parishes, since St. Martin's has already been combined with Fourteen Holy Martyrs. I'm trying to do what the diocese needs.

I can't help but compare my present situation as pastor of two or three parishes with Holy Name, the parish I grew up in. They had four priests in one parish plus the brothers. Things have changed drastically in one generation. You don't see the word used much, but we are "downsizing" even though we don't want to admit it. This is a new experience for the Church, and not a pleasant experience.

Another comparison I can't help making is the difference between my life as a priest in Brooklyn and my life as a priest in Central or South America. In Paraguay and in the Dominican Republic. I was free to visit homes and evangelize. I did not spend any time on maintenance, rather I helped to develop a co-op with the people in town and bring people back to Church.

The diocese where we were in the Dominican Republic was so international that we were actually proud to be Catholic and American. We had priests from Spain and Ireland. We had brothers from Germany and sisters from Spain and Canada. There were American Franciscans and the missions from the Brooklyn Diocese and Rockville Centre. It was quite a group, young and enthusiastic. It was the Church of the 60's and 70's. It was the Church of the poor. We may not see their like again. I was proud to be part of it.

I wish I knew where we are headed in Brooklyn. Is the answer to keep merging parishes and to give every priest a dual assignment? I don't think so. I think we have to energize the Catholic people to assume more responsibility for the running of the parish and to evangelize as the Pentecostals seem to be doing. They are the fastest growing Church in the U.S.

When I talk about evangelization I mean to ring doorbells and to openly speak about our faith to others. The diocese now has a Pastoral Planning Office with each parish setting up its own pastoral plan. People are being encouraged to state frankly what they like and dislike about their parish. I think something good can come out of this effort. Also, if Jehovah's Witnesses and Pentecostals can share their faith in Jesus and the Gospels, so can we.

We are certainly not going to have the vocations like we had in the 40's and 50's but this will make us use our laypeople more.

Note: John accepted the assignment to St. Martin of Tours on a trial basis. He quickly realized that the work of being pastor of three parishes, even with an assistant, was too much for him. He has now been assigned to the parish of Our Lady of Mercy. A former pastor, standing in the midst of large areas of buildings torn down in the name of urban renewal, leaving only the Church standing, called the Church "The Little House on the Prairie."

I came to St. Martin's knowing that it was big, especially with the addition of Fourteen Holy Martyrs and Our Lady of Lourdes. When the list of vacancies came out from the Diocese, I saw that Our Lady of Mercy was listed. At my age and with my health, I recognized that a place with one building was much more attractive than a place with eight buildings. There will be two priests in St. Martin's and I will be alone as pastor of Our Lady of Mercy. There once was a time that St. Martin's had four priests. Fourteen Holy Martyrs had three. Our Lady of Lourdes had three. So where today we have two priests there once were 10 covering the same area.

Of course more people were coming to Church in those days so more Masses were needed. It was a much different time. We have three Masses on a Sunday, two in Spanish, one in English. There is one Sunday Mass in our Lady of Lourdes. Twenty years ago there were five or six Masses here and four or five at Fourteen Holy Martyrs and more at Our Lady of Lourdes. Baptismal registers and Marriage registers show a decrease everywhere. That's just the way things are. We are not growing, we are "downsizing." We do the best we can.

A lot of people inquire about my health. I'm grateful for their concern and their prayers. I've had Non-Hodgkins Lymphoma for the past seven years. I'm certainly not sick every day. I go to Sloan-Kettering and they monitor my situation. I get cat-scans. My energy level is good, considering my age. I get up early every day. I go up and down stairs. I'd like to get off me as the subject, and address our situation as a diocese with an ever-worsening priest shortage.

As we priests get older and older we cannot continuously take on more and more responsibilities. My frustration, as we have spoken about before, is the frustration of having large buildings that are in constant need of repair. I don't have the resources to repair them and it looks, especially to the older parishioners, that things are going "downhill." In the future we will have St. Martin of Tours Church and Our Lady of Lourdes Chapel. But we are not quite there yet. The site of Fourteen Holy Martyrs has been sold to a Protestant Church and the Catholic School is now a Christian Academy. But the area is still ours to evangelize.

I still think that the future of the Catholic Church is in the hands of the laity, not full-time people but part-time people who function like deacons. Last week the Brooklyn Tablet had the pictures of 36 deacons going to be ordained and another 16 Spanish deacons to be ordained next week. We will soon have two priests in St. Martin's and three deacons. The deacons will out number the priests. How's that for the "signs of the times"?

I have to say as we talk about married lay people and married deacons that celibacy has worked for me. I did not leave as a young priest and now 41 years later I'm happy I stayed. I look at my brother and brother-in-law and I see how much time each dedicates to the Church and works full time. I wonder where we are going to be in five or six years.

I do think we should move to optional celibacy. It has worked in the Eastern Church; why would it not work for us? I'm not sure if celibacy is keeping men back, it might be but from my experience I'm just not sure. I do not hear any bishops calling for optional celibacy.

The debate on celibacy is remote for me. Issues like prayer are more relevant. I try to pray in spite of the fact that I am very busy. Prayer has become more important as I grow older. I pray the Divine Office every day. I spend about half an hour in prayer, including the Office, each day. I make time for prayer. Early morning is the best time for me. I go on retreat once or twice a year. I say Mass each day.

My life is simple. I get a good salary. Money is not a problem for me. I try not to be ostentatious in the car I drive or the vacations I take. I am aware that the people I serve are poorer than I am.

For me as a priest, my focus is on the Mass and the Sacraments. I would like to be as I once heard the priesthood described as "teacher of the Word, minister of the Sacraments, and leader of the community." Even in Latin America, where, as you know, I spent many years, most of our time was taken up with the celebration of Mass and the administration of the Sacraments because the numbers were so great. I think that lay people should be in charge of the social ministry of the Church and the priest be in charge of training lay leaders and being the leader of worship. It gives all of us plenty of work to do.

CHAPTER SEVEN

REV. DONALD J. KENNA
Pastor, Priest-Worker and Scholar

Donald J. Kenna died June 6, 2006. These interviews were conducted with several of the people who knew him well. In going through his papers, they came across notes Don had written about his experience as a Priest-Worker.

LINDA PITTARI

Linda was a good friend of Don Kenna's for many years.

Donald Joseph Kenna was ordained a Roman Catholic priest in 1964. When he graduated from the minor seminary he didn't go to the major seminary at Huntington, Long Island. Instead he went to the major seminary, St Mary's in Baltimore, Maryland. It was there that he met Gene Walsh who played an important role in implementing the reforms in the Liturgy after Vatican II. Father Gene Walsh and Don Kenna remained good friends for the rest of their lives. They were kindred spirits. He also met at St. Mary's Father Raymond Brown, the famous scripture scholar. Donald and Ray Brown remained good friends. Ray Brown had a great influence on Donald both in the seminary and for many years after.

Don's first parish was St. Francis Xavier in Brooklyn. He then went to St. Ambrose in Bedford-Stuyvesant a few years later, and he spent the rest of his life among the poor in the Bedford-Stuyvesant and Williamsburg areas of Brooklyn.

It was at this time that Donald began to explore the history of the Priest-Worker Movement in France, and he discovered that their idea of priesthood was very much the same as his, that the priest should not be spending so much time in the rectory but should be out in the world living among the people. His desire to be with the people and get out of the rectory drove him, with the approval of Bishop Mugavero, to accept a job with Con Edison, New York's giant power utility company, where he worked for 21 years. He felt priests should take greater responsibility for their lives. Don felt that priests allowed themselves to become too dependent on the institutional church. In his view, they are given absolute job security with benefits. They have a guaranteed income and housing. Most have a maid and a cook. Someone comes in to make the bed and fold the laundry.

So not only did Donald take a secular job, but he rented a couple of rooms in a nearby tenement. He moved out of St. Ambrose rectory and set up his own apartment. In fact, he first moved out of the rectory and then he found a job. He had to cook and clean for himself. He had to take greater responsibility for himself like anyone has to take – all of this with the approval of Bishop Mugavero. Don had concluded that given the discrepancy between the lifestyle of clergy and parishioners, he could no longer live in the rectory or accept money for his priestly services. He never took a stipend for any Mass, baptism or wedding that he might celebrate. He did not want any connection between money and the sacraments. This is not because he had his own means of support from Con Ed, but because he believed in it. The result of this was that Don became even more in touch with people's lives and grew as a person and as a priest.

Don used to say, "The only real sin is not being open." Don grew through these experiences. He went to St. Ambrose every day and said Mass as needed, then he would go to his job at Con Ed. Don saw Con Ed as his ministry. Everyone knew he was a priest. He was in contact with people who had little or no contact with their local church. The only reason he left Con Edison was his health. He had a heart attack in 1996. He resigned at that time. He had become pastor of All Saints in 1989 and he was working only part time at Con Ed, one to five, about four hours per day. Sometimes he would work a night shift (6 to 10 at night) in order to give himself a full day in the parish. If it were not for his health, he would have remained at Con Ed. For 21 years, he was both a priest-worker and a parish priest. He was also the spiritual director of Marriage Renewal and he taught scripture at St. John's University. He did a lot. He was never bored.

Don Kenna believed in Jesus. He studied Jesus. He taught himself Greek so he could read the New Testament in its original language. He was very serious about this. He taught himself Hebrew so he could read the Old Testament in its original language. He was consumed with a desire to know this unusual man from Nazareth with his message and determined actions and the conflicting reactions of people with whom he came into contact. For Don, every story about Jesus brought a new way of looking at life.

He was very loving. He made time for people. He had the gift of connecting to people. He had a fabulous sense of humor. He was kind and gentle. He was casual. He rarely wore the Roman Collar. He would say, "People should recognize me as a priest, not by what I wear but by what I do, how I live." He was a wonderful preacher because he studied and lived the Gospel message in his own life. He was interested in everything and everyone. He never became indifferent to the pain of others. He was equally comfortable with the rich and the poor. It was never about his own agenda, it was about the needs of others. He totally believed in the Kingdom and in the Resurrection.

I recall one particular conversation about the priesthood which he actually wrote about. He talked about joys and dark days, days of doubt and frightful fears and the indescribable but growing sense of a "power" in his life. He felt connected to the Holy Spirit. He realized the priesthood opened up a ministry that would not have been possible if he were not a priest. On the other hand, he sometimes felt inhibited by the bureaucracy that was placed on him in his role as priest.

He was very intense but he had what I call many "moments of happiness." He was happy when he returned from a recent three-month sabbatical at Tantur in Israel, because he saw some hope there in the Sabeel Movement that is trying to bring Jews and Palestinians together. He was at peace. He had been renewed. He believed so much in social justice issues. He planned to have a Sabeel meeting in NYC in October. He died before he could attend the meeting.

Don died of a massive heart attack at his beloved All Saints Church on June 6, 2006. It was 6 months after his return from Israel.

It is consoling to know he died without pain and in peace. He was looking forward to retirement and had plans to study and write. Unfortunately, that didn't happen.

We have set up the Donald J. Kenna Fund to keep his memory alive through his work of educating youth. Our goal is to create a scholarship fund for young people in memory of Don.

WALTER MITCHELL

Father Mitchell is a priest in St. Margaret Mary's in Brooklyn. He was a close friend of Don's.

I met Donald about a year before he was ordained. He was at a party with seminarians and priests and we started talking. Whatever I said impressed him and we started a friendship. Donald invited me to do something at his first Mass. I knew him for 42+ years. We talked a lot. We became "cruise buddies." I was in St Agnes and he was in St. Francis Xavier, neighboring parishes. This was in September 1965. In 1966 we went on a cruise together, hence the phrase "cruise buddies."

Donald was so multi-faceted. He would be furious at false luxury and at the same time, he would enjoy a fine meal which cost money. Also, he had great love for anyone who was the victim of injustice. Great love for people who were weak. But, no love for the weaknesses of "systems." He was intensely involved in causes. He had the great gift of seeing things black and white and not gray. He had an unusual tolerance for an individual's fallibility. He could and did forgive.

He was so charismatic. I would introduce someone to Donald and immediately he was the center of attention. He radiated a gift. He would ask people questions as if he didn't know the answer. He would wait for people to answer the question that he already knew the answer to. He would play that game with me and sometimes I'd fall for it. I'd be out to dinner with Donald and a third person and I'd go back to my rectory and just leave the two of them together talking and Donald would have never met this person before and they would be speaking for hours. Unless he was in an argumentative state, which he sometimes became, he made the other person the great star of the moment.

Donald devoted a great deal of time to studying the scriptures. Many guys have to look up things, he did not. It was an intrinsic part of who he was. He knew the scriptures.

Donald's great gift was to make people feel liked and loved. The individual was the center of attention and then his biases and all the black and white would disappear. When it came to individuals, he was a great believer in individual freedom. When it came to groups it was different.

Other gifts – acceptance of individuals; ability to proclaim to the simple, downtrodden and poor that they are good and great and that they deserved more than this world has given them.

He had a particular gift that many of us do not have and that's the gift to vacate. To be able to say, I am going to disappear for a day or two and do nothing but read and think.

GEORGE MCLAUGHLIN

George McLaughlin is a long-time friend of Don's. He is currently a Guidance Counselor at Central Falls High School in Providence, R.I.

I met Father Kenna when I was a kid in St. Francis Xavier parish. I almost forgot what led to our meeting, and was reminded of it after Don's funeral. He was talking to some boys in the parish, shortly after he arrived as a newly ordained priest, about the capacity for every one of God's children to be saved. The kids said, "There is one guy you will never save and it's Georgie." So he searched me out. I was already in deep trouble. I was 15 years old, on drugs and in gangs and everything else that went with that. I was a troubled kid from a broken home. One of his gifts was searching for lost sheep, like me.

The relationship changed as I got older. He became a real friend rather than someone who was helping me. Father Kenna helped me turn my life around though. He came to my graduation ceremony at the therapeutic community I had spent two years in. He helped me get into Queens College, and he visited the campus with me for the first time. The list goes on and on. He was someone who didn't take credit for anything. He was always facilitating things, always opening a door for me or helping me to open it myself and then backing off and letting me go through it. He was someone I could rely on for advice and throughout the more than 40 years that I knew him, that never ended. The relationship went from the streets in Brooklyn to being the best man at my wedding. I wanted him to be the best man to show him that he was my friend, not just my confidant. I went from a high school drop-out and in jail to having three degrees and five teaching certificates and teaching at three different levels; from being anti-religion to eventually becoming a traditional Catholic with two kids who have grown up with the faith, and are attending Catholic schools, and a wife who has had a similar spiritual transformation into the life of the Church. I give Don credit for this, for getting me started and supporting me on the biggest journey of my life.

As I think about Don, he's very hard to describe. The more I knew him the more I didn't! He could be enigmatic. The thing about Don was that he was always someone who was a witness to God's ability to change your life.

What a privilege it was to have known him, our wonderful brother.

My sense of him was that he was looking beyond the space we were both standing in. He had a great insight into other people. He could see goodness in people, goodness that most of us couldn't see. As I got older and went back to the Catholic Church and renewed my faith, I came to believe that he had an immense belief in the power of Jesus Christ and his ability to change people's lives. The picture I painted in my eulogy for him at his parish, All Saints, a picture of me standing at the rectory door in the middle of the night, a troubled, confused and almost hopeless boy, ringing the doorbell for Father Kenna, illustrates that.

The thing that kept him going was his tremendous Faith and his great sense of what people were capable of. He viewed people with a tremendous amount of compassion. He gave people a lot of room. He was patient. He let God work in people's lives, not letting his own ego interfere. He had an unbelievable capacity to wait for the fruit after the seed was planted. When I would mention someone's name, he would sigh and say she or he is such a good person. The sigh was a recognition of the person's virtue and suffering. He had a great sense of what each person he met was suffering. He touched so many people because he had that capacity. I know now it came from his great faith in God.

He often reminded me of the quote from Mother Teresa when she was asked how she had helped humanity. "I don't help humanity," she replied. "I only help one person at a time." That was Father Donald Kenna's passion, helping one lost soul at a time. Even though he had a world view, institutionally and politically, that was not his heart and soul. It was that kid or bum or disaffected Catholic, ringing the doorbell in the middle of the night. That's why he never complained about those things. He complained readily enough about bureaucracy and egotistic personalities in the Church and other institutions, but he never complained about the troubled and forgotten.

There was a whole inner world of Father Kenna that I didn't see because personally, Father Kenna was a shy person who was, at the end of the day, very private.

He was a great listener. He had a great sense of how to create community out of dialogue. That's why he called our weekly or monthly get-togethers in Brooklyn or other parts of the city, "dynamic seminars." A bunch of us would go out for dinner and sit for hours talking about issues and ideas. He absolutely loved those conversations, always seeming to discover something new during every one.

In the end, he was a great man! For me he was like a father and then an older brother and then a friend.

JIM HEANEY

Jim was a very good friend to Don over many years. He and his wife Pat live in California but always had dinner with him when they came back to the east coast at least twice a year. Jim is the President of his own company.

I've known Don since I was sixteen years old – when he first went to St. Francis Xavier. I lived on Carroll Street, one of the "Carroll Street Boys." Don had a way of changing people's lives through his "presence." At St. Francis, Don got together twelve of us boys from Carroll Street. He called us the "Twelve Apostles." He started a weekly meeting and what we talked about was our lives and how God fit in. He even organized a Passover Seder in the lyceum one year. It's still a vivid memory in my life and in the lives of all my friends who attended.

During that same time period, Don went to Selma, Alabama, and joined in the march with Martin Luther King. He never told any of us, but one of the guys noticed his picture in the crowd of marchers with Dr. King in *Life* magazine. I believe the Civil Rights Movement had a profound impact in the direction of Don's life. He spoke out often and courageously on injustice when most people in and out of the church were in denial.

Don absolutely changed my life. Everyone has a thought about the first person they met that they saw Jesus in. Don was the first person I saw Jesus in. He was different. It wasn't that he did a lot of great things, but as Mother Theresa would say, he did a lot of things with great love.

He was famous for doing his midnight walks. You could walk in the streets in South Brooklyn - whether it was the gangs or drug addicts or the homeless, he knew all of them and he knew every single person who walked through the doors of Saint Francis Xavier Church. If you looked at Don, you would have to say that's the measurement of what a priest should be.

He would always make time for you, no matter what the problem was. He always showed up when people were having bad times. He was truly a very special person. He had a tremendous connection to people, as they had with him. His natural instinct was to serve. With Don you really felt you were a part of the church. The church wasn't the place that told you all the things you were doing wrong. I moved to California two years after I met Don and for the past forty years, I've made many trips back to New York and always put aside the time to visit with Don.

MICHAEL WEST

Michael is a young man from All Saints who knew Don well.

I met Father Kenna in the winter of 1992 on the steps of All Saints' Church. I was waiting for the Church to open when a tall white man shouted to me to wait for him, he would be back. Although we had never met before, we spent several hours talking like old friends. I was surprised that he was so interested in my life. I later understood that was how he was. He wanted to get to know you, be a friend and find ways to help you. I was born in this country and then returned to Nicaragua to grow up. I came back to the United States at 17 years old without a family, a job or a place to live. Father Kenna gave me guidance and even walked with me from store to store to find a job. He believed in me, encouraged me to learn English and go to college. He helped me with my papers and gave me a vision of my future. He was the first person who thought that I was "wonderful." No one had ever said that to me before. In 2000 I graduated from Baruch College with an Accounting Degree. In 2005 I got married and in 2006 bought my first home. None of this would have been possible without Don Kenna's support and influence. He became the family I didn't have.

CHAPTER EIGHT

REV. JOHN MULHERN

MARRIED PRIEST

My background is clearly Irish working class. My father was a cop. My parents emigrated from Ireland in the 1920's. I grew up in Maspeth, Queens. Everyone in the neighborhood was Catholic. There was a strong sense of the value of priesthood. To become a priest was strongly encouraged by family and friends. I went to Catholic elementary school and high school (Most Holy Trinity). I tended to be fairly religious. I went to Mass most mornings. In that neighborhood with me going to Church frequently, it was kind of expected that I would go to the seminary and become a priest. In those days, if a young person practiced his or her religion and was interested in religion it was expected that he would enter the seminary and she would go to the convent. That's what young people did.

If you were "religious" you became a priest or a nun. There were few other avenues open to you for service. My decision to become a priest was not influenced by any single person. It was more the culture, the environment, the family. But not a single person.

I was ordained for the Diocese of Brooklyn in May 1964 and I left the active ministry five-and-a-half years later.

After ordination, I was assigned to learn Spanish at the Language Institute at the Catholic University in Ponce, Puerto Rico. When I returned to Brooklyn I was assigned to Transfiguration Church in Williamsburg, Brooklyn. One of the curates with me was Bryan Karvelis who had a strong influence on the parish, on our work and on me as a young priest.

The ministry was clearly with the Hispanic community, working at first with the Puerto Ricans and then over the last few years with the Dominicans.

We established a very strong youth program. For youth who were in the Church, there were such organizations as the Young Christian Workers (YCW) and the Young Christian Students (YCS). For youth who were in the neighborhood but not active in the Church, there were "social clubs." I was very active in youth work, giving retreats, running the youth center. I would be in the youth center two or three nights a week, meeting with young people in the youth program. Youth work was central to our ministry. Then there was the whole aspect of "community service." I got involved in issues like housing, voter registration and the Civil Rights Movement. So it was a very active ministry, not only in the sacramental sense but also in the community sense.

Eventually we trained lay leaders, especially among the youth. We brought in speakers, set aside training days and organized workshops around the theme of Christian leadership. The youth themselves took more and more responsibility for the running of the youth program. I was happy and felt good about the work I was doing.

In spite of this I clearly made a decision to get married, that I wanted to be with Luz. I could not have had a relationship with Luz and be honest as a priest.

The process of leaving was fascinating. I went to see the bishop. Bishop Mugavero was very kind and fatherly. I told him I wanted to think about leaving for a year before making a final decision. He offered to send me to another parish where I could earn a little more money and have more free time to think about things. I went to a new parish, St. Jerome's, and in five days I knew I did not belong. I realized I could not be happy there. So it made the eventual leaving very easy for me. Bishop Mugavero, unintentionally, helped me to find out what I should do. I stayed in St. Jerome's a few days and then I went back to the chancery office and told them I wanted to take a leave of absence. It was that simple. No one tried to talk me out of it.

What makes my situation interesting, and maybe a little different, is that I married a girl from the parish (Transfiguration). We stayed in the parish and raised our three children there.

Luz and I decided that after we were married we would try to live in or near Transfiguration parish. Some people, a minority, found it difficult and were upset. Not the majority. For the first year or two we lived in the neighborhood but a little outside Transfiguration parish. Now remember, a large number of people from the parish, bus loads, had attended our wedding in St. Paul's chapel at Columbia University in Manhattan. More importantly, Bryan Karvelis attended the wedding and was very supportive. This really gave us credibility in the minds of many people. His role was crucial for our acceptance by the community. So by and large, from the very beginning, there was a great deal of acceptance.Then as we began to attend Mass in Transfiguration, the people became more comfortable with me as a married priest with a wife and family and some continued to call me, "Padre Juan" as some people still do today.

The bishop was more concerned about my living near or in the parish than the people were. It was not what he preferred. Bryan, on the other hand, encouraged it. Then it turned out that the parish had a house to sell and Bryan offered it to Luz and me. It was right next to the Church. We bought it. This meant very clearly that I was going to be involved in the parish. I was not only coming back to Mass but coming back to share in the ministry of the parish. I took a job in the community where I was able to help people get jobs and find decent housing.

For three years I worked out of the Mayor's office. As a priest I had been very involved politically. I had been a delegate to the Democratic National convention. I worked in Richard Neuhaus' unsuccessful campaign for congress. I had made lots of contacts. I had many political friends and access to many people, including commissioners. I worked out of the Mayor's office on issues such as affordable housing for seniors and jobs for newly arrived immigrants. I found the work exciting and satisfying.

I had a leadership role in all of the social and community work of the parish but not in the sacramental or liturgical work of the parish. Bryan and I had a clear agreement that I would not do anything liturgical in the parish. It was Bryan's way of not upsetting the people or the bishop's office and not putting in danger the work I was doing in the parish. Bishop Mugavero would always ask for me whenever he visited the parish and he never gave Bryan a hard time. It worked out well. I did not offer Mass but I had a free hand in the Gospel work of community service.

I was very involved in community politics and social service, especially child care, which was and remains a great need in the community. I considered it a form of ministry, maybe not priestly ministry but certainly a form of ministry, a form of service coming from my baptismal calling. But Luz was not happy. She wanted me to get out of politics completely and only do community work. I was smart enough to take her wise advice. Our growing family needed a father with a steady income, not an income that could change with every election in November. I got out of politics and resigned from the staff of the Mayor's office.

Eventually I became the director of "Nuestros Niños" (Our Children). Nuestros Niños was a very large child agency with over 200 employees, most of whom were women. I learned to be very flexible and to listen to the needs of the women on our staff, many of whom were single mothers taking care of their own children as well as the elderly and the sick at home. They just could not handle an eight-to-five day, five days a week. Their needs required more flexible scheduling and I tried to arrange this. Coming from strict factory work, they thought I was God, or close to it. We developed great loyalties and they were always ready to go the extra mile whenever I needed them. It was good management and it worked out well. We were able to satisfy the needs of the children as well as the needs of the staff.

Nuestros Niños was a Day Care Center. We had 135 – 140 children in the pre-school program during the day and 60 – 70 children in the after-school program from 3 p.m. to 6 p.m. Our initial budget was more than $300,000.

I have been asked if I considered my work with Nuestros Niños as "priestly" work. I don't consider myself an ordained priest representing the Catholic Church. I see the Church as highly imperfect and I am not responsible for it. I like it that way. I am willing to take some responsibility for the Gospel being preached and the freeing message of Jesus not die out. One of my greatest fears is that, in first world countries, young people will give up on the Gospel because they have so many problems with the institutional Church that it is not a good vehicle for communicating the Gospel message. I would like to play a role in keeping the Gospel alive, particularly among young people.

I have to start with myself. I must try to live the Gospel in what I do, in how I live my life. Then I must talk about Gospel values with others. I'm a part time professor in the Urban Semester Program for Cornell University. The program operates out of New York City. Each semester I bring the students to Transfiguration Church and we spend the day walking through the parish, taking about values and sacred space and the role of the spiritual in our lives.

My heart is in Transfiguration parish and I presently give two or three days a week, as a volunteer, to run the social service program in the parish. I like what I do there. It's a large agency. Last year we had almost 10,000 clients with about 15 paid staff and another 20 volunteers. We do immigration work, youth work, and housing, work with seniors. We run a homeless shelter and a food pantry. A lot of stuff and I enjoy it! By and large over the past few years I've been able to use my contacts to raise enough money to keep each of the programs afloat. It relieves Bryan of a great deal of worry and responsibility. This whole social service program, all of which was inspired and founded by Bryan, is called "The Mission."

The work I am doing now is very important. We save a lot of people. I find enormous peace and fulfillment at the Mission. I don't need the priesthood. What I'm doing now is right for me. As I said, I like what I'm doing, part-time volunteer trying to help people.

More and more I am seeing that the critical question is not whether a man is celibate or married. The critical question is whether this man, celibate or married, is able to relate to people. The ability to relate to people, to empathize with people, to feel another's pain, to be compassionate, this is what is critical for a pastor, not whether he is married or celibate. I did not find that celibacy gave me a greater ability to relate to people just as I found that marriage did not increase my capacity to relate to people. You relate to people because of who you are as a person, not according to marital status. But let me be clear. Mandatory celibacy is wrong, even sinful.

Mandatory celibacy is part of the reason why some celibate men do not relate to women and therefore do not respect women or listen to them. Many of us, and I certainly include myself, entered the priesthood with a great deal of sexual immaturity. We had not dated girls. We did not know girls. We were encouraged to avoid girls. We did not grow up in a normal way in regard to our relationships with women. It was understood that women were evil because they could make us lose our vocation from God. Mandatory celibacy might have made sense in the middle ages when the hierarchy did not want Church lands given to the sons of the local clergy. It does not make sense today. St. Paul condemned the idea that celibacy was required of Church leaders.

There is no theological justification for mandatory celibacy. Optional celibacy, yes. There is some justification for it. There is no sound scriptural, traditional or theological basis for mandatory celibacy. This is why I said that mandatory celibacy is wrong, even sinful.

I have no problem with the ordination of women, but I have one great fear, that if women are ordained, even fewer men than now will present themselves for ordination. This has been the experience of most Protestant Churches that have been ordaining women. Of course I do not present this as a reason why women should not be ordained. If the presence of women at the altar or in seminaries is an obstacle for some men, that is their decision. It should not deter us from doing the right thing, ordaining women.

We've tried to live a simple married life in Williamsburg, a depressed area. We've stayed in touch with family and friends, some of whom thought we were foolish to live in a poor and potentially danger-ous neighborhood. We developed some strategies of our own like being sure when the children left the house they always had some money with them in case they were confronted by someone demanding money.

Luz grew up here and was poor. She wanted to be sure that not only did our children (two boys and a girl) have enough to eat and to wear but also that they had the latest educational toys and games. I thought we had overdone it, but looking back I guess she was right. We never drove fancy cars or went on expensive vacations but we borrowed money to send the children to the best schools we could find. Two went to Harvard graduate school and one is a lawyer.

I personally have tried to live simply but money keeps following me. We bought a house in a poor area, Williamsburg, and yuppies are mov-ing into the neighborhood and paying a great deal of money for houses. So our property values keep increasing. We bought a trailer home in a depressed area of the Catskills years ago and now the area has become very desirable. I am far better off financially than I ever thought I would be, all of this while trying to live a poor and simple life.

I was never completely comfortable with the Fraternities in the parish. They tended to be a little elitist. So I never joined a parish Fraternity. I was a member of a priest Fraternity but when that broke up as people went their own ways, I never joined another Fraternity.

My spiritual life is rather traditional. I'm able to go to Mass four or five times a week. I try to find quiet time each day for prayer and reflection. During the night I often get up and pray. It has been a great help to me. I love this quiet time and during this quiet time I have received many thoughts and insights on what I can do to make my life better and to make better the lives of those around me. When you are busy, it is just too easy to do the wrong thing: to get angry with your children, to get angry with other people, to dismiss others, to not listen with an open mind, to take a wife for granted. At night, when all is quiet, I have received remarkable insights on what kind of a husband or father or friend or guide or human being I should be. This is my most prayerful time.

My life is hectic but creative. I want to keep growing and learning. Sometimes I think I do burn out. People renew me. Bryan, of course renews me, working with Bishop Joe Sullivan on housing issues renews me, supervising Jim O'Shea renews me. He is a young Passionist priest who came to Transfiguration because "I want to work with the poor" bringing with him a great sense of humor and a brutal honesty about the institutional church. He is still with us. All these people and many more, renew me. I like being part of a team. I am not out there by myself. If I make a mistake, a bad judgment, there is always someone to point this out to me before any real damage is done.

I read but not as much as I would like. I read both religious and secular material. I read magazines: National Geographic, St. Anthony's Messenger, Maryknoll Magazine.

I enjoy retirement. It has given me greater control of my time. I'm happy to be volunteering rather than working for a salary. Of course it helps to have a pension, Social Security and a TDA. We give away a fair amount of money each month. We can support various projects because we actually have more money than we need to live on. This gives us control of how we want to spend it. We send money to Missionary Sisters in Africa, to Transfiguration parish, of course, and many other causes. Luz and I give away about 10% of our income. I thought we would need more money in retirement than we actually do need. Also Luz has worked longer than we thought she would. So we ended up with some money we can just give away, no strings attached.

CHAPTER NINE

REV. JOSEPH A. NUGENT

IN OUR FATHER'S HOUSE

I was ordained in 1971. I grew up in Our Lady of Guadalupe parish in Brooklyn and I was influenced by the priests of the parish. I saw the kind of work they were doing and I thought that I'd like to do that. I saw the influence they had on people's lives. It seemed like important work. Then there were the sisters in the school. They always spoke so highly of priests. All of these elements formed an atmosphere that made me think of becoming a priest.

I went to Cathedral Prep, the minor seminary, for two years, right after graduating from elementary school. I went for only two years because after two years I was asked to leave. My marks were not so good and I was going out with a Jewish girl. Some one reported me. I was advised to leave Cathedral. I was told that I did not have a vocation to the priesthood. I enrolled in a public high school near my home. I graduated from there and worked in a bank for a year.

In the back of my mind I had the feeling that I should try again to become a priest. I applied to the Society of African Missions. I was accepted and went to their seminary in Massachusetts. I stayed there for three years. I left and finished up at St. John's University.

I thought I should try Brooklyn again. I applied and was accepted into the major seminary at Huntington. I was ordained four years later.

The seminary was very intellectual, very academic, not practical at all. To make matters worse, it was the time right after Vatican II. We had no textbooks since so much of theology was being revised as a result of the Council. We were given a massive number of articles to read. We called it "Article Theology." It was a tough time to be in the seminary with so many changes in the Church, especially the liturgy.

The seminary was definitely not practical in terms of living out the priesthood. I do not feel I was well prepared by the seminary for the life of a priest in an urban diocese like Brooklyn.'

After ordination I went to the Language Institute in Ponce, Puerto Rico, to learn Spanish in order to work in a Spanish speaking parish. The whole experience was a disaster for me. I lasted about five days. I was both homesick and physically sick. I didn't like the atmosphere there. It was not for me so I came back home to Brooklyn.

I met with Bishop Mugavero and he assigned me to work for the summer in a camp on Long Island run by the Diocese of Brooklyn. It turned out to be a very positive experience of priesthood. All the kids were inner city kids and it was wonderful! They prepared me for inner city work.

I got a call from the personnel board in September that they had an assignment for me at Our Lady of Victory in the Bedford Stuyvesant section of Brooklyn. Since I was newly ordained and this was an inner city parish, they asked me if I would accept the assignment before it was officially announced. I told them, "Yes," I would go but they had to assure me that if I had problems they would come and get me right away. Even after the positive summer experience I was still a little afraid.

It turned out that I stayed in Our Lady of Victory for 21 years. I fell in love with the parish and the people. They really formed me as a priest. They taught me how to be a priest. They taught me to be one of the people. They taught me to be among the people but also to strive for holiness, to be present to the people but also to be present to God. They taught me to reach out on a social level to the needs of the community. I started to see the homeless in the area, the abandoned buildings, the alcoholism among the people. I felt that I had to come up with some solutions. I started to attend the Alcoholics Anonymous (AA) meetings that were held in the school.

I began reaching out to the community, to the fellows sitting on the park benches. They would ask for help and I had to find out what kind of help was available and how to connect the "help" with the person looking for the help. I hooked up with the detox unit at Swedish Hospital and until it closed in 1975 I brought many people there. It was a very successful program but I saw that when people finished the program they went back on the street and fell into the same habits. They needed an alternative.

Our school had closed and I asked the pastor to give me a few rooms and we would start a shelter called, "Our Father's House." He said, "sure," and gave me four classrooms. We started with two guys.

When they were not attending the clinic they had to be in the shelter. We gave them meals, a clean bed, showers and a safe environment. We quickly grew to 25 men. That was the maximum number we could handle and supervise. We gave them hope. They didn't have to return to the streets. They had a place to stay.

The men started to keep sober. Sobriety was an important part of the program. The men had to attend AA meetings almost daily. Over a period of 12 years, we served and sheltered over 1,500 men and we never accepted government funds. We lived by donations.

I sent out a monthly newsletter to the names on my Christmas list. People were very generous to us. We collected about $150,000 a year and that just about covered our expenses. We accepted no government money at all. When the sisters moved out of the convent, we moved in and had a much better setting for a shelter.

Our next step, once some people had achieved sobriety, was to run the program all day long. Our guests stayed in the shelter 24 hours a day. We provided all the supervision. There was one man, Jesse, who had worked for me for over a year and in whom I had complete confidence. Jesse and I ran the program. We both went to Fordham for a Masters degree in human development and adult education. Jesse ran the program from 9:00 a.m. to 5:00 p.m. I came in at 5:00 p.m. and stayed overnight until 9:00 a.m. the next morning. I moved out of the rectory and moved into the convent with our guys. It worked very nicely for many years. Quite a few men achieved sobriety. No one was allowed to be on welfare. If they came to us and were on welfare, we got them cut off.

We ran it like a seminary. They were in groups all day long. They had a work period each day during which they did physical labor, mostly around the Church. Our Lady of Victory did not have to hire anyone. We got the parish off the subsidy. Jesse was the only paid staff in the program.

Neighboring parishes collected food for us and raised money for us. We ran a 90-day program. If, after 90 days, people wanted to continue living with us they had to have a paying job and give ten percent of their weekly salary to the shelter as rent. I actually saved this money for them and gave it back to them as a savings when they were finally ready to move out. No one could stay more than a year. If they started to drink again or take drugs again, they could not return to the shelter.

Eventually, I ran into conflict with the State. They said I had no license and therefore I was running an illegal operation punishable by a year in jail or three years probation. They also said I was keeping people in the shelter against their will for 90 days. I told them to look at the size of our guys. No one could keep them here if they did not want to stay. Bishop Mugavero and I decided to close the shelter because complying with all the State regulations and mandates would have destroyed the heart and soul of the program. It closed in 1987, but I did not leave the parish until 1991.

I moved back to the rectory and we offered the convent to John Fagan from Little Flower Children's Services. He needed a place for six babies with AIDS and for the women taking care of them. The program of working with babies with AIDS relocated and we gave the convent to Mother Teresa who turned it into a residence for unwed mothers. That's what it is right now.

During this whole time the people kept forming me, encouraging me to reach out to the drug addicts, to the alcoholics, to the sick in neighboring hospitals. I was constantly with the outcasts, with the sick, with the rejected by our society. I realized how comfortable I was in that environment. I accepted them and they accepted me.

I received criticism from some people who accused me of bringing "the bums onto holy ground," but most parishioners defended and encouraged me and my ministry to the rejected. However, I did maintain a sacramental ministry especially to the sick in the hospitals that I visited every day. Also, I worked in the religious education program. The development of good liturgies was always important to me. We produced some liturgies that were truly magnificent, sometimes lasting as long as two hours.

In 1991 I was transferred to St. Rita's in Long Island City. There were both an English speaking community and a Spanish-speaking community. The bishop told me my job was to bring them together. "Easier said than done." I knew I had to learn Spanish so I went to the Language Institute in Douglaston, Queens. I stayed in St. Rita's for five years. I never did bring the two communities together.

In 1996 Bishop Daily asked for volunteers to go to the Dominican Republic. I volunteered but I lasted only three or four days. Like my experience in Puerto Rico, my experience in the Dominican Republic was a total disaster. I was homesick again. I was with very good people but I was not happy. I missed Brooklyn terribly. Thank God I came back because I got very sick and I needed open heart surgery soon after I returned.

When I recovered, I was then assigned to St. John the Evangelist parish in Park Slope that had a large Mexican community as well as some older Irish and Italian families. I loved it. I stayed there for three years and in 2001 I was assigned to Presentation in Brownsville. I've been here about five years now.

Life in Presentation has been different. Once again I found two separate and distinct communities: one Spanish-speaking, the other English-speaking. The Spanish-speaking community is mostly Puerto Rican. The English speaking community is mostly Black and makes up about 2/3 of the parish. My focus is to build up the parish.

The focus here for many years had been social outreach to the poor. That is great but the place was falling apart, physically and spiritually. There was nothing going on here. The two communities were at each other's throats. The Sunday liturgies were terrible. I'm putting all my emphasis on the parish and building up the Church.

I'm alone here, no other priest. No cook or housekeeper. I have a secretary.

When I moved here five years ago I was the pastor of two parishes, Our Lady of Loretto and Our Lady of the Presentation. There was another priest, Freddy Rozales. He chose to live at Loretto and I chose to live in Presentation. Theoretically, we were both to work together in the two parishes.

The way it worked itself out was that Freddy stayed at Loretto and emphasized a ministry to the Spanish-speaking community and I stayed in Presentation and emphasized a ministry to the Black community. Very few people went to Mass at Loretto. There seemed to be more hope in Presentation. Then the floor caved in. I mean that literally. The floor in the Church of the Presentation fell in. No one was hurt. We had to move to Loretto for three months but it gave me the chance to talk to the people about building up the Church, not only the physical building but the Church as the Body of Christ. I commissioned them to go out and build up the Church, the people of God. It worked. More and more people started coming to Mass in both

English and Spanish at Presentation. However at Loretto fewer and fewer people were attending Mass.

I did a study of the situation and I sent a report to Bishop Daily. I recommended that we close Loretto (I had a potential buyer) and put the emphasis here in Presentation. Most of the people in the Chancery office agreed, but Daily said, "No." He said he wanted to maintain a "pastoral presence" in the area around Loretto. I said to him, "your pastoral presence is going to kill me."

I then suggested that the Bishop make Freddy the administrator of Loretto and me the pastor of Presentation and we would stop the running back and forth. They accepted this division. Each parish would be autonomous as it is today.

Loretto is still functioning, but it is very small. They get about 30 people at the English Mass and 25 people at the Spanish Mass. Here we get about 250 at the English Mass and about 125 at the Spanish Mass. I try to keep the Church open 24 hours a day. I've done this in every Church I've been assigned to. I've kept them open day and night, even in the inner-city.

The Church has not been vandalized or if it has, it is minor stuff. The people respect the Church. You'll find people in the Church praying at different times of the day or sitting, relaxing, even sleeping. The Church is a refuge, a sanctuary for them. Isn't that the way it is supposed to be? I think so.

Also, I'm happy being celibate. I've chosen to minister in poor and often violent communities. I couldn't bring a wife and children here. I couldn't work in these communities with a clear mind knowing that I had to take care of a family and protect them from violence. I wouldn't want to expose my family to the dangers on the streets here. This is a violent area. The rectory does get broken into from time to time. I would be afraid for my family.

However, while I am not married, I am also not lonely.

I stay in touch with a lot of priest friends. I go out to dinner with them. I take vacations. If I find myself getting lonely, I get on the phone and call a friend and make arrangements to go out to dinner or go to a movie. Or I'll do things. I'll go out and work in the garden. I'll do something physical around the Church, especially in the warm weather and I'll meet people. People see me out there and they stop and talk. I get involved. That is my best medicine for loneliness: get involved.

I have a variety of friends, male and female. I can be very honest and open with them. Or to use your word, I can be "intimate" with them.

We all need intimacy in our lives. If we do not have it in healthy relationships, we will try to find it in unhealthy relationships.

There have been a lot of changes in my priesthood over these past 35 years.

When I first started out in Our Lady of Victory, I was more than traditional, I was conservative. Even mentally, I was definitely in the conservative mode, concerned about orthodoxy. Whatever came out of the Vatican was the truth for me. Over the years I learned that things are not as black and white as I had once thought. As I got involved in people's lives I saw that not every one can practice all the ideals the Church teaches. I saw people living together not because they did not want to be married, but because they couldn't get married under our immigration laws. I became more open to the human situation.

I see myself as a man of the community but, because I am white living in a predominately black area, I am also set apart. There is a difference, as much as I would like to think there is no difference. I am here in this community, but I feel the separation because I am white. Putting aside the racial difference, I think the priest should be both immersed in the needs of his community but also set apart by being a man of prayer, a man who puts aside time each day for prayer.

As I look back over my 35 years in the priesthood I guess what stands out in my mind is the shelter program, reaching out to the homeless and the addicts in Our Lady of Victory and providing alternatives to drugs and alcohol and living on the streets. I am also proud of working with the sick in the hospitals, especially in St. Mary's which had become a center for AIDS patients at the height of the AIDS crisis. I went from being afraid of them to becoming close to them as they were dying and praying with them because they had asked me to be there. Being sick myself, with open heart surgery and then having part of my stomach removed, has made me very sensitive to people who are sick. My brother and both my parents had stomach cancer so I have to be very careful and take care of my health. As I said, this has made me sensitive to those in poor health.

I am also proud of the liturgies we have been able to develop in the different parishes I have been in, especially getting the children involved. They are invited to come around the altar and feel comfortable there. We want every one, children and adults, to participate and they do. We have just started a children's choir to complement the adult choir. We have a liturgical dance group that dances on special occasions.

Our liturgies are long. The English mass takes a good hour-and-a-half. The Spanish liturgy goes on for about an hour. I preach at the

English mass for about a half hour. We try to make the liturgy the high point of the week. People are volunteering to come in each Saturday and clean the Church. We want them to take ownership.

I look for ways to praise people. Every one likes to be praised and recognized. It shows in our finances. When I came here, we were receiving from the diocese $120,000 in subsidy a year. Now we do not get any subsidy and we have $50,000 in the bank. We used to get about $1,000 on a Sunday. Now we get $3,000.

I'd like to return to the celibacy issue. I want to be sure that I'm clear and that you understand my thinking about celibacy.

I'm not opposed to optional celibacy. I don't see why it wouldn't work. But it might not work everywhere. It might not work in areas that are violent. If I had married I would have had a very different ministry then I've had. If I were married and had children, I would have sought out a more middle class parish where the safety of my family would not be an issue. My point is that while I am not opposed to optional celibacy, if I had married I would not have had the same ministry I've had as a celibate. I hope I'm clear on this.

There is more to spirituality than celibacy.

I knew that when I went to Our Lady of Victory I had to be there "as one among you." If the people I am serving are poor, I had to be poor also. When I was running the program for the homeless, I did not take a salary from Victory so I might identify more with the poor. I lived off the donations that came in and I literally lived and slept with the drug addicts and the alcoholics in Our Father's House.

I do believe in poverty. I do believe in living simply. I do not believe in living better than the people I am serving. But poverty is not just for me. We are all called by the Gospel to share our goods with others, especially the poor in Third World countries.

Closer to home is the priest shortage. It affects me and all priests in the sense that I am called to do more work, like covering more than one parish or helping out in another parish because the one priest who is there is going on a vacation. More and more priests are living alone. It is the trend throughout the diocese, not just the inner city. Some priests do not want to live alone, so they live with another priest in his rectory and commute to the parish in the morning. Other priests, like myself, choose to live alone.

The sexual abuse scandals have also affected all of us in a negative way. It is very, very, very upsetting. It has affected me terribly. I know many priests who have been placed on administrative leave. They are devastated. The bishops have treated these men terribly. I am disgusted. There are about 35 priests in Brooklyn who are caught in this "administrative leave" business. I am in touch with many of them. Many are depressed. Some are suicidal. The bishops have turned their backs on all of us. The bond that used to exist between priests and their bishop has been broken. The bishops have opted for "cruel and unusual punishment." Tribunals should be set up quickly. Cases should be heard. Priests should be able to bring counsel and defend themselves. Bishops should be bound by the decision of the Tribunal.

What is difficult for me is to find time to pray.

I used to think that I could get away without a lot of formal prayer. "My work is my prayer," I used to say. It was the heresy of activism. I realized something was missing in my life. What was missing was prayer. I now spend a day a month in prayer at Douglaston with Danny Murphy. At the end of the day we go out to supper. I try to go periodically to the days of recollection sponsored by the Diocese. I go on a retreat each year for a week. Last year I went twice.

I walk four miles a day because of my heart. I use the time to pray the rosary as I am walking along. It takes about an hour each day. People see me and greet me. I do some spiritual reading each day and I pray at least parts of the Divine Office each day.

I spend some time in quiet prayer each morning before the Blessed Sacrament. I try to remind myself during the day that I am in the presence of God. I no longer believe that "My work is my prayer." Prayer is my prayer. Of course, I celebrate the Eucharist each day. It is important that I take the time to renew myself or else I will burn out quickly and easily.

I read. That renews me. The hour outdoors spent walking renews me. I feel the lack of it when I don't do it. I go out with priest friends frequently. I go out with lay friends, female and male, periodically. I go out with couples, husbands and wives. My brother has ten children so I have plenty of nieces and nephews to keep me busy. I stop in to see them. I continue to study Spanish. I go to the movies. I enjoy a good movie. I am active in the Right-to-Life movement. It has given me a greater respect for all life, for all stages of life. It renews me.

The priesthood has been good. If given the choice, I would do it all over again.

CHAPTER TEN

REV. JOHN T. PEYTON

A MINISTRY OF JOY AND LONELINESS

I was ordained for the Diocese of Brooklyn in 1961. I have been a priest for 45 years.

Right after ordination I was sent to the Catholic University of Puerto Rico to study Spanish. This was at the time of the large immigration of Puerto Ricans to the United States, many going to Brooklyn and New York. We studied at the Language Institute set up by Msgr. Ivan Illich. Ted McCarrick, who would eventually become the Archbishop of Washington, D.C., and Sister Thomas Marie were there – all unique people. The Institute had a very dramatic effect on me as a person. I met priests and nuns who took the Gospels seriously and who were preparing to spend their lives in ministry to immigrants from Puerto Rico.

I had just come out of the seminary where the major theme was to obey rather than think. Now at the Institute we were challenged to think. Illich was extremely controversial. He made you think. He challenged the bishops of Puerto Rico on the contraception issue. Not even his patron, Cardinal Spellman, could protect him.

For Illich, "the pill" was a matter of conscience, not of legislation. We went out on weekends to hear confessions and we had to counsel people whose bishop was saying contraception was a mortal sin while the newspaper were quoting Illich that contraception was a matter of conscience. It was very challenging for a young priest who had been taught to obey his bishop.

I had been influenced very early in my training by the idea that the Church must minister to the needs of people. I worked summers, while in the seminary, with the Trinitarian Sisters at the Dr. White Settlement House and signed up adults for classes for Baptism and First Communion. At the same time we found out about other problems they might have with welfare or housing or drugs or with their teen age children. The Trinitarians Sisters were very influential in my life, especially Sr. Thomas Marie.

I also worked these summers for Catholic Charities in the Family Division doing basic social work. Now all of this was before ordination. I did social work during the day and visited people in the housing projects at night for "Convert Classes." For me, it was all part of "trying to make a difference," of being Christ to all people. I was happiest working with the poor. I found the work both interesting and challenging. All these experiences – with the Sisters, with Catholic Charities, and the nightly visits in the projects – all helped to form me. They had more of an effect on me than I had on them.

I returned to the Diocese of Brooklyn from the Language Institute in Puerto Rico in September of 1961 more or less fluent in Spanish. I was assigned to St. Agnes parish in downtown Brooklyn. Joe Panapinto had been assigned there a couple of years before me.

I wasn't given any time to get my feet on the ground. I was immediately thrown into parish work. Besides our duties in the main Church, Joe and I were assigned to run Sagrado Corazon (Sacred Heart) chapel in the middle of an all-Latino section of the parish. Within six months of my assignment to St. Agnes, Joe left the priesthood. We had had a good working relationship. but now I was even more on my own without any help or support. I was already starting to feel isolated.

I was in charge, by myself, of the Spanish Apostolate in St. Agnes parish. This really meant running the chapel and forming groups there. Because I was the young curate, I was also given all of the youth work as well as all of the Spanish work.

On a Saturday, I might have a 9:00 a.m. Blessed Virgin Sodality meeting for teenage girls followed by religious instructions in Spanish followed by a Baptism and a wedding at 3:00 p.m. and confessions from 4:30 to 6 p.m. Then there was youth work at night. It was too much. I tried to bring the work of the chapel and the work of St. Agnes together but I was not very successful. I was dealing with two distinct cultures. I had two heavy loads, one in the chapel in Spanish and the other in St. Agnes in English. It was all work, work, work and I felt I was always falling behind. I rarely took a day off to be with friends. This helped to further isolate me. I admit that I was at fault. I didn't call my friends and they hardly ever called me.

I was in St. Agnes for three years when Bishop Jack Snyder, Director of the Personnel Board and the auxiliary to Bishop Mugavero, called me down to see him. There were problems in Our Lady of the Presentation parish in Brownsville and they needed more help. He asked me to go to Presentation. I was happy with the thought of a change and felt it would be a new beginning for me. I needed a change and I looked forward to working with other priests of my own age again.

Presentation was an enormous parish. There was the main Church plus a mission Church, Our Lady of Mercy, plus a Center called Good Shepherd. Initially there were three priests, including myself, assigned to Presentation parish. Two priests were assigned to Our Lady of Mercy and one priest was assigned to Good Shepherd.

But assignments and living conditions changed as most of us moved out of rectories and into apartments. Over the years nine priests would be assigned to work in the area. Of the nine, five would eventually leave and marry. We were given a great deal of freedom and relationships developed. These were very exciting times with a lot of experimentation in ministry and life style. Most of us in Presentation parish lived in small groups of two or three in an apartment. Others, like myself, would eventually choose to live alone while others chose married life.

I moved out of the apartment and moved into a new Center we had opened up on Ralph Avenue called, as you might expect, the Ralph Center. It had been broken into several times. I thought if I was living there it would cut down the break-ins. I lived there for 12 years. I was lucky that I never got hurt. There was a cafeteria in the Center so I could always get a sandwich and a cup of coffee, something light.

We worked in the field of housing and tenants' rights. We persuaded the Board of Education to allow us to form an experimental school district that gave real power into the hands of parents. We worked with welfare recipients. We, along with some lawyers from outside of Brownsville, developed CUSA (Christians United for Social Action) which eventually became Christians and Jews United for Social Action.

We developed youth programs and religious instruction programs. We taught everything from English as a Second Language to how to become a nurse's aide. We visited homes during the day and held meetings at night. Back at the apartment we might be up until two or three in the morning as someone was pouring out his soul about ministry or whether to pursue a relationship or remain celibate. We were exhausted but happy. We felt we were "making a difference." It was an exciting time and it may never be duplicated.

Bishop Mugavero gave us a great deal of freedom. He assigned Father Ed Burke to be the pastor of Presentation and to keep an eye on us. Ed was a great help to us. He had a wonderful reputation in the diocese and he had the full confidence of the Bishop. He formed the link between us and the Bishop. We were developing new ways of being priests, living in apartments or Community Centers with an emphasis on social ministry and outreach to the poor.

We started slowly in the development of our ministries. We began with the traditional view of what a priest does. We organized religious instruction classes for adults and children. We baptized and prepared people for the sacraments. We developed good liturgies with lots of participation.

Soon we were into breakfast programs and we started to get more involved in schools. We worked with the Black Panthers. In fact they ran the breakfast program out of Ralph Center. Their idea was that children needed a good breakfast so they would not go to school hungry. We went from there to organizing ESL (English as a Second Language) classes. We set up training classes so that young people could become nurse assistants and have careers in the health field.

Of course it took years for these programs to be conceived and then developed. We had ideas and space. The city, state and federal governments had the War on Poverty money. It made sense to work together. Eventually the program at the Ralph Center where I lived became a five million dollar operation. Most of the participants were Haitian. At one point we had six Centers open day and night.

I started to do some work with the Haitians who were moving into the area around Ralph Center. The people were there and I started to celebrate Mass for them at the Center. It just happened.

I spoke some Creole, not as well as I spoke Spanish, but enough to get along. I said Mass in French. I preached in English and the deacon translated into Creole. The deacon became a crucial person for me in the Haitian Apostolate. We would have a few hundred people for Mass every Sunday.

The other priests in Brownsville were focused on the Puerto Ricans, but I began to devote more time to the Haitians. I marched with them in demonstrations in Washington, D.C. and I worked with the US Conference of Catholic Bishops on what was called the "resettlement" program. As Haitians made their way into the country, often illegally, they had no jobs, few contacts and no housing. They needed to be "resettled." I worked closely with Haitian priests who came over with the people and I developed a great deal of respect for them.

The work with Haitians grew and grew. At one point we had six separate buildings or centers in Brooklyn and Queens. We developed more and more training programs leading to real jobs. We tended to concentrate on young Black men who had little skills. The ESL work expanded among the Haitians who were anxious to learn English. It became a very big operation with many components. The program was known as BHRAGS which stood for "Brooklyn Haitian Ralph and Good Shepherd." I was the Executive Director. Eventually, I resigned and a former Jesuit took over for me.

The program had become too big and too much for me. The program did not need a priest as executive director. I had developed it and I had seen it grow. It was time for me to move on. I had been Executive Director of BHRAGS for about 15 years. We had many programs and I felt we were doing God's work of feeding the hungry and training the poor.

Unfortunately, the program came into trouble over money. The new Executive Director squandered a great deal of money, but the real blow came to the program when it was discovered that the person in charge of the money was stealing from the State and Federal money we were receiving. In time all six centers closed and all the programs dismantled. It was a very hard time for me, to see the programs I had worked so hard for come to an end.

I moved out of Ralph Center and lived by myself in an apartment. But the apartment experience began to come apart as some priests left to marry and others moved back to parishes and rectories. Then I was assigned as the pastor of St. Rita's in the East New York section of Brooklyn. I've been here for almost 25 years

I don't get out much during these past years. I have a bad back. The parish is my family. I'd hate to leave them but it will happen some day. We have a new bishop, a lot of unknowns.

We have a large school, about 600 students. We have the Big Brother program and a big adult education program with about 200 people in ESL classes. I'm back into establishing training programs. Besides the ESL program we have GED classes, immigration work, Domestic Violence Prevention programs, and a lot of leadership training. But most of all, I work with East Brooklyn Congregations (EBC) where I am the Co-chairman along with Dr. Youngblood.

I don't see the priest as one set apart. Unless I am immersed in people I will never know the joys and the pain that priesthood is all about. I have to be with people so that their struggles become my struggles. I can only bring new life and hope to people if I am part of them and with them.

The more I am with people, the more amazed I am of their faith and how much respect they have for good priests. Even with all the sexual abuse scandals, people still have a deep respect for the priests they know.

The group of priests I don't have much contact with are the younger priests. I don't know many younger priests. But I do know they seldom come to me for advice or to pick my brain. I guess they would consider me an "old man" with little to offer. We both lose. It's interesting. I remember the respect we had for Ed Burke years ago. He was much older than we were, but in many respects he was our mentor.

The big question we all have is this: when I retire will there be a priest to take my place? I hope so. I hope a priest will come and the people will gather around him, as they did with me. What form the Church will take remains to be seen. But it will go on, maybe in ways much different from the Brownsville experiment. I am not apologizing for the work we did in Brownsville. I feel we accomplished a lot. Look at the gains we have made in providing affordable housing through the Nehemiah project.

As I said, I'm presently the co-chair of the East Brooklyn Congregations and the treasurer of the Nehemiah project. I've been involved in EBC almost from the beginning. We've already built about 3,000 homes. They are all single-family homes and the average mortgage is $400 to 500 a month. The homes are valued at about $130,000. The people have a yard, front and back, much to be proud of. The homes have two stories with bedrooms on the second floor. We have made a real contribution.

We are still working in schools and on very local issues. When we have a clear case of police brutality, we will demonstrate against it. A lot of social action work is still going on.

I am very proud of our parochial school. It is in good shape. Enrollment is good. We have two classes in each grade. We have about 600 students in the school. I attribute our success to good leadership. To put it simply, we have a great principal. Also we took in children, Black children, years ago when other schools in the area would not take them. Our tuition is $1,400 per year, per child, but many are on scholarship.

I don't get into the school much these days, not as much as I would like. We have a good principal, good leadership. I'm wise enough to leave him alone. Also my back prevents me from climbing stairs.

We have a lot of things going on here. We do immigration work. We have religious instruction classes. We go on retreats.

If I had to choose a single person who influenced me a lot, especially in working with the poor it would have to be Sister Thomas Marie, a Trinitarian nun and a great lady. Looking back there was also Ivan Illich and Joe Fitzpatrick in Puerto Rico. It was a blessing to have known them. They certainly had an influence on my life decisions. I also should mention the influence of two priests of the Diocese: Msgr. Bryan Karvelis and Msgr. John Powis. They've had a great influence on me.

I am no longer working with the Haitians. We have very few Haitians in St. Rita's. I have been out of the Haitian Apostolate for many years. I had to give all of that up when I moved to St. Rita's. But there are great Haitian priests who minister to the people. I worked closely with one in my early years, Fr. Guy Sansaricq who was recently named Auxiliary Bishop in Brooklyn.

I have tried to live like the poor, no matter where I was assigned. I am now near the age of retirement. There is Social Security but it isn't much. I did not contribute when I was younger. My Social Security is about $400 per month. That along with help from the diocese will be it. I am more and more conscious that I will be on my own, for the most part.

I have a place to go to in retirement. I have a small apartment in Rockaway Beach. I don't want to live in isolation but, my back hinders me from getting around.

I worry about being alone. I worry about having nothing to do in retirement. Most of my good friends have died. My mother and father are dead. I went to my sister's for Thanksgiving. It was nice; better than being alone.

Since I'm talking about being alone I'd like to say a few things about celibacy, which is what most people want to talk about anyway.

Celibacy has made me available to people, probably more available than if I were married with a wife and family and had those responsibilities. On the other hand, and it is a big "other hand," could I have used the support that marriage gives? Yes, certainly. Celibacy gave me space but it has also brought isolation and very little feedback on how I was doing. I might have had a more effective ministry if I had more support and feedback. There is not much satisfaction in doing everything alone. There is something to be said for intimacy and partnership and sharing.

From what I've already said, I guess it is pretty clear that I think celibacy should be optional rather than mandatory.

We've lost so many good people because of mandatory celibacy. So many priests have had to leave their ministry merely because they wanted the companionship and intimacy of marriage. In my own life, I'm wise enough to know that I need people and that I'm too much alone. I know that when I feel down and alone, I should reach out to other priests, even if only for a brief chat on the phone. I know what to do but very often I don't do it. As they say, "The spirit is willing but the flesh is weak."

I've made plenty of mistakes in my life and one is that I've never had a real vacation or a set weekly day off. For most of my ministry I've been in situations that if I weren't there, Mass would not be said. So if I went away it would have to be after the Masses on Sunday until Saturday night before the evening Mass. Now, looking back, I realize I have not taken enough time away from work to renew myself. There is also the aspect of money. I never had enough money to take a real vacation and I wouldn't ask my family for money. I have the parish for my family and I find peace and joy being with the people of the parish. This is how I've survived.

I would like to think that the heart and soul of Jack Peyton is the Lord. I pray that I make a difference and build the kingdom of God in our world and that I be open to the Spirit of God working within me. That's what I seek.

CHAPTER ELEVEN

REV. JOHN J. POWIS

COMMUNITY ACTIVIST

I was ordained in 1959 so I've been a priest for 47 years. I've mostly worked in poor parishes. The first, St. James, the Pro-Cathedral of the Diocese of Brooklyn, was actually a mixed parish with poor people living in the projects, middle-class families living on the side streets and more affluent people living in a development called Concord Village. It was a nice mix of people.

Even before ordination, I worked in the area with the Trinitarian Sisters during summer vacations from the seminary. We tried to visit every family in the parish. After ordination and after studying Spanish in Puerto Rico, I was assigned to the same parish. In those days there were four priests in the parish and so I was "on duty" only one-and-one-half days per week. This left plenty of time to visit families in the parish.

We tried to bring together the people from the projects with people from the side streets and people from Concord Village. The parish school was a great help. We were not entirely successful but we did have kids from the different groups in the parish playing basketball together and, more importantly, parents from the different groups attending meetings and socializing together. As I said, the parish school was a great help in bringing adults and children together.

My next parish was Epiphany in Williamsburg. I was there for only eight months before I was assigned to Presentation parish in Brownsville. I would stay in Presentation for 25 years.

I spent my first few months in Brownsville just walking around the parish. It was huge! and 100% minority with about 60% Hispanic and 40 % Black. The priests in the parish were overwhelmed. There was no Spanish Mass and no outreach to the Black and Latino communities. I recruited some young people and we cleaned out the church basement for youth work. There were so many children in the parish that we had religious instruction only for children in 5th grade and above. There was not enough space to handle the younger children. The Board of Education gave us, free of charge, three schools in which to run summer programs. One summer we had 16 Christian Brothers and 43 nuns working with us. The former pastor at Epiphany parish, Fr. Ed Burke, joined me at Presentation and called it an "experimental parish." The importance of Ed's assignment to Presentation parish became clearer as time went on. The Bishop allowed us to experiment because Ed was there.

There were eight priests assigned to Presentation parish. Six of us lived in apartments, visiting families, and working on such issues as housing and schools. It was controversial. Not everyone agreed with what we were doing.

I always believed, right form the start, when we were seminarians, that we cannot deal with a person as religious or non-religious but as a human being, as a whole person. If we are going to talk to people about religion, we must also talk to them about where they are living, how they are living, the quality of schools their children attend, their personal problems, etc.

I got involved in schools because when I came to Brownsville, children went to school for only ½ a day. They went to school either from 8 a.m. to 12 noon or from 12 noon to 4 p.m. There were different teachers for each session. There were two principals in each school. There was chaos.

We then found out that in other districts there were "underutilized schools." There were schools in middle class areas that were half empty. One summer we went door-to-door and registered 1700 children whom we said should be bused to these "underutilized schools." In Glendale, a middle-class neighborhood only about 10 minutes away, the parents made it clear that they were not accepting any children from Brownsville. They meant, of course, that they were not accepting any Black or Latino children. So we had to bus children to other schools 40 – 45 minutes away. And the children were not accepted when they got there either. One of the saddest experiences I've had as a priest was going on a bus with children to their new school only to have men and women throw eggs at them and at their school buses. It was awful.

As a result of this experience we formed an independent demonstration school district known as Ocean Hill – Brownsville. The New York City Board of Education allowed us to form our own district with the eight schools closest to Presentation Church. We worked closely with the State Education Department as well as with Bernard Donovan, Chancellor of New York City schools and with Mayor John Lindsey and his deputy mayors. Initially we had a good relationship with the teachers union (UFT) and with its president, Al Shanker, and his assistant, Sandy Feldman. This good relationship did not last long.

We held elections to put one parent from each of the eight schools on the Ocean Hill – Brownsville school board. All the parents were black or Hispanic. Rhody McCoy was selected by the board as superintendent of the new school district. State Commissioner Allen gave the board great leeway in the hiring of supervisors and teaches. The UFT could not accept this and called for a citywide strike of all schools (except the eight in Ocean Hill – Brownsville). The strike lasted eight weeks, until the end of November. It was a very tense time in the life of the city and in my life.

After 25 years in Presentation in Brownsville, I was assigned to St. Barbara's in Bushwick where I have been for the past 15 years. One day a Lutheran pastor, John Heinemeier, visited me. We talked about bringing into Brownsville a professional community organizing team. We both agreed on the need to do community organizing through the Churches.

In a short time we had raised $250,000, mostly from the Lutheran and Episcopal dioceses. We brought in the well known community organizing team known as the Industrial Areas Foundation (IAF) and formed the East Brooklyn Congregation (EBC). We started by organizing around the simple issue of "street signs." There were no street signs in Brownsville. They had been all torn down and traded for drugs. But eventually we turned our attention to the issue of housing.

Now 12 years later we have built 3,000 single-family homes with another 800 homes ready to start construction soon. We call the whole project "The Nehemiah Homes." It has been a great success. Bishop Mugavero of the Diocese of Brooklyn loaned us millions as seed money to start the housing work. All this plus interest has been paid back

EBC is also working with the IAF in the formation of small high schools in cooperation with the NYC Board of Education. We now have three small high schools in the Bushwick area. Each school has about 500 students, almost all of whom go to college. But we do not skim off the best students. We take any youngster we have room for. Last year in one of our schools we had 800 students applying for 125 seats. We have complete control over the hiring of teachers and supervisors. We are presently working closely with the new NYC Chancellor – Joel Klein. It has been a very exciting time.

In my vision of priesthood, social ministry is part of my priestly ministry. They are not two different things; I don't believe they are separate. If I can provide a good dynamic liturgy on a regular basis and still be able to take care of the physical needs of the people, both as families and as individuals, then both aspects of the priesthood become one. I am both celebrating the sacraments and reaching out to people in need. It is all pretty simple.

People keep asking me why are so many inner-city parishes in decline with less than 200 people at all of the Sunday masses? But there are four parishes here in Bushwick with more than 2,000 people every Sunday. Why? These four parishes have good liturgies and they take care of people's needs during the week. St. Bridget's deals with immigration. We send all our immigration cases to them and they send their housing problems to us. We all work closely together. All four parishes not only provide good liturgies and religious instruction classes but also provide the people in the area with social services. It is all part of the good news that God is Love.

I realize that I am known as a community activist. That is just part of my priesthood. It is all one. This is my deep belief. It has been my belief from the beginning. First and foremost a priest has to be a person closely connected to the Eucharist. A priest has to be the person who makes liturgy the number one thing that happens in the parish, the person who is concerned about the participation of the people at Mass and all the things we were taught about liturgy from Vatican II.

I have done a RCIA (Rite of Christian Initiation for Adults) for 22 years. This program teaches and trains adults to become better informed Catholics and to receive sacraments. We have always had, here in St. Barbara's, over 40 adult baptisms each year. We do about 500 child Baptisms each year and we conduct a personal interview with each family before the Baptism. These baptismal interviews are the best way of getting to know a lot of parishioners. It is an opportunity to invite people to get married in the Church and receive sacraments. All this is part of the "cultic model" of priesthood. It has to be balanced with a ministry that addresses the social needs of the people.

I am still trying to put it together. Not long ago I realized I could not do the administration of the parish with all its buildings and still find the time to meet with people without putting my health in danger. It was time to retire. I can not do at 72 what I was able to do at 32.

So I have picked out 25 families with multiple problems and I am in contact with them. Then there are a number of people who are seriously sick and I visit them. I spend one day a week at St. Barbara's so the young priest who took my place can get away for an overnight. Then I have been doing a lot of work with housing. I have identified certain buildings in the area and I am working with the tenants.

Poor people are being put out of their homes as landlords rehab buildings and sell them to middle-class people who are able to buy or rent. There is no new construction being built for poor families. More and more families are going to shelters because the way the system works is that if you are in a shelter for more than two years, you are eligible for Section 8 housing. In the meantime, the family is almost destroyed as it gets moved from one shelter to another. This is sad for a country that spends a billion a week on the war in Iraq.

I had two young interns who worked with me on housing issues over the summer. We went out and visited families most nights between 4 p.m. to 8 p.m. So many people are afraid because they are from Mexico or Ecuador and are here illegally. They are overcharged and they pay it because if they don't, the landlord says he will report them to immigration. As I walk around, most people know who I am and they ask me how can they get their marriage "blessed," or how do they get their child into religious instruction. It all comes together.

What I am doing now is building a "Church without walls." What I hope to do is to use my contacts with people throughout the city and bring them together for prayer, discussion and maybe Eucharist. It is all part of a "Church without walls." What I am concerned about is how young priests will take to this "Church without walls" concept. Young priests are being trained very differently than I was. Some share our vision of the priesthood but, as far as I can see, the majority are being trained to be professional men in charge of the sacred. Social action gets referred to others. Here is an example: people are asked to submit to the rectory the addresses of buildings where drugs are being sold. These notes usually come to one priest. There are other priests who could handle it, but they do not consider it "priestly work." By and large, I do not see the majority of young priests interested in social ministry. Some are, but not many.

I try to live a poor life and spend as little as possible on myself. I don't have a savings account. I don't own a car. Of course, not owning a car may not be all virtue because it frees me to use public transportation which is very good in this city. I know all the routes of the subway system and I don't have to worry about traffic jams or parking spaces. I'm better off without a car.

I do not buy expensive clothes. I don't worry about it. The people know that if you are voluntarily working in poor areas that you do not have many material goods and to a certain extent they admire it. They tend to be generous and look after their priests.

I want to say a few things about the present discipline of mandatory celibacy for priests of the Latin rite.

First of all celibacy is a gift, but if you do not have the gift, it becomes a great burden. Celibacy has been a gift for me. I've had many opportunities not to be celibate but I've always decided not to pursue them. But it has been a struggle, a constant struggle. Most people do not have this gift. A faithful married priest in inner-city parishes is even a greater symbol than a celibate priest because so many people are involved with random sex. The sooner the hierarchy recognizes that celibacy should be optional rather than mandatory, the better off we will be. In my own life, celibacy has been a struggle but a good thing and fruitful. Does celibacy make a priest more available than a married priest would be? I am not sure. I think that if I were married with a family, I would be just as available as I am now. I do not think celibacy, of itself, makes a man more committed or available. It depends how you use it.

I'm finding that as I grow older celibacy creates loneliness in me. I notice people holding hands in the street and if I see intimacy in a movie, it creates a loneliness in me. The sacrifice can be a good thing. But celibacy is not for everyone. I do not think the priesthood should be limited only to celibates. It is not the reality of things, but unfortunately that is how we still operate. I am not too sure that all priests, especially the younger ones, are fully committed to celibacy. I have a definite suspicion that priests do the best they can. Many are not celibate but continue to be priests and do good work. Bishops project the image that all priests are celibate. It just isn't true.

One thing that has helped me persevere in the priesthood is that I've had the good fortune of being a member of the Fraternity of Charles de Foucauld, for about 35 years. We've always had a solid core group of six or seven Catholic priests along with a couple of Lutheran pastors. Some of the priests are from different dioceses and one is from Maryknoll. If I go through a day without a good hour of prayer, I feel there is something missing. I try to spend an hour in prayer every single day. For me, the best time is in the morning but I do not always get to it in the morning. I learned, while on a 100-day retreat in Santa Fe, how to make the day's experience into a prayer. So if I do not spend an hour in prayer in the morning, I do it later in the day, like around five or six in the late afternoon before things get to be too hectic. In this way I can bring to my prayer the experiences and the people I've seen during the day, their struggles and hardships. It does not take away but adds to my prayer. It helps me to connect in a prayerful way all that has happened during the day.

So I've always had the blessing of a group that is able to give me guidance. We meet monthly and we reserve the afternoon for a "Review of Life." We try to be very open and honest with each other and to give each other advice and direction. So I get monthly spiritual direction not only from one person but from six or seven priests who know me very well. The Fraternity has been a great blessing in my life.

Recently, I wrote a short article for the *Brooklyn Tablet* entitled "The God of Summer Surprises" reflecting on my work over the past summer in St. Emeric's parish on the Lower East Side of Manhattan. I wrote:

"That night when I got home, I was going to watch the Mets and the Yankees - it was the last week of the baseball season – but instead I sat in a chair and began to cry. It wasn't a sad or angry cry. It was a cry of thanksgiving for the gift of my wonderful three months with God's people at St. Emeric's and my 30 years of being a member of a priests' fraternity with Bryan Karvelis. I realized that all my activities of this summer and all my actions of my previous 46 years of inner-city ministry were only fruitful because I rarely failed to spend an hour every day in quiet adoration in the presence of the Blessed Sacrament as prescribed by our priestly fraternity. As the heat and humidity of this past summer fades into the cool, breezy days of October, I am so grateful to the God of summer surprises!"

CHAPTER TWELVE

REV. JAMES RICHARDSON

FILS DE LA CHARITÉ

Apparently, it takes me a long time to be sure about my decisions. I've been accused of that. Ever since I can remember, as a kid who was an altar boy and a choir boy, I had this desire to be a priest. I went to the minor seminary and then to the major seminary and I was sent to Louvain in Belgium to study theology. I remember thinking when I went to Louvain everything was "black and white." I mean literally, black and white. I was dressed in a black suit and white shirt. If anyone should ask me a question, I had the answer, either in my head or in a pamphlet in my pocket. Everything was clear, black and white. When I returned to Brooklyn, four years later, everything had become gray. Nothing, or almost nothing, was black or white any longer.

I mentioned Louvain. John Hyland and I were there in the years before the Council, 1959 to 1963. John XXIII was elected in 1958 and the Council began in 1963. Many of our professors at Louvain were chosen to be "Periti" or "consultants" at the Council. They would come into class and say, "I'm not going to be here for the next two weeks. I have to be in Rome." We were always happy about that. We were especially happy when the Canon Law professor announced that he was going to Rome and classes would be discontinued until he returned.

In the meantime we spent the summers in Europe on vacation. In fact the rule was that if you were sent overseas to study, you were not allowed to come home for the summers – too expensive. So my four summers were basically spent over there. Remember, each summer we had about three months off. Now the American College, where we were, required that six weeks in the summer had to be spent in what was called "parish time." We had to find some parish or religious community where we could spend six weeks and then we were free to travel the rest of the time. The reason for spending time in France the first summer was to practice our French.

We were interested in what was going on in the French Church at that time. There was so much going on in liturgy, theology, and pastoral work. We were not allowed to stay in the city of Paris (too sinful, I guess), so we wrote to different parishes around Paris and asked if we could spend six weeks there. We received a number of positive responses. But the one that interested us the most was a parish in a South Western suburb of Paris and we spent the next six weeks of our first summer there. The pastor belonged to a religious community, the Sons of Charity, but the two assistants were diocesan priests. It was a diocesan parish because the Sons of Charity didn't fully staff it.

The Institute, that would become the Sons of Charity, was founded in 1918. The founder, Jean-Emile Anizan (d.1926), had become very involved with the working class, especially those working in the factories in Orleans. He saw how hard they worked and how poor they were. .He developed a passion to spend his life working with and living with the oppressed workers in France. He became involved in the social problems of the day, especially in the development of a "workers' movement". Pope Leo XIII's encyclical on the rights of the working class had been issued in1891. Anizan felt strongly that the way to reach the working class youth was through the family and the way to reach the family was through the parish. In many ways he was a man ahead of his time. He founded his own religious community called the Sons of Charity (Fils de la Charite).

We have a threefold emphasis; 1) to be saints; 2) to be sons of God who is charity (love). So for us "charity" means God, not social work; 3) to live and work together in community and to be efficacious in our apostolic work which includes parish work, but not limited to parish work. The founder's idea, which the community is just getting back to, is to have brothers as well as priests in the community. When the Sons of Charity were founded there were an equal number of brothers and priests. Then over the years we began ordaining only priests. We are now returning to the founder's original vision and we are accepting candidates for both the priesthood and brotherhood.

For it to work brothers and priests have to treat each other as equals, not with the brother doing the so called "lower" work and the priest doing the so called "higher" work. We are now trying to get back to that, being sure, as I said, that we treat each other as equals, all as "Sons of God who is love."

We've gone through our own ups and downs with both liberal and conservative leadership over the years. During World War II a number of our guys were held in captivity for long periods of time. After the war, things really took off. We had a great number of vocations and remember, this was all in France at that time. There were parishes with teams of five and more. Some joined the Priest Worker Movement and worked in factories in order to reach out to the working class that had become so alienated from the Church. Even though the Priest Worker Movement was officially disbanded by Pius XII in 1954, some of our priests continued to work. We have a small percentage of our priests involved in work, although most are now in parishes. There were some conflicts within the community. Some priests emphasized the parish as the place of evangelization while those in factories wanted nothing to do with parish.

The conflict is now pretty much resolved. It is not a matter of "either/or" but a matter of "both/and." During the week workers are in factories and at night and on weekends they are home in the parish.

Let's get back to our story. When John Hyland and I visited this parish outside of Paris we found out, unlike here, that the suburbs are the poor areas and the cities are the affluent areas. So in the summer of 1960 we found ourselves in a poor parish with a member of the Sons of Charity as pastor. His name is Father Francis and he became a great mentor for John and me. He took us around to meet other members of the Sons of Charity. He told us about their work and their history. John and I both saw the need for this kind of work among the poor in Brooklyn. But knowing the situation in Brooklyn at that time, we did not see how it would be possible. We both struggled with it. Should we return to Brooklyn or not? John continued on to priesthood but I was not sure. I turned down the call to Deaconate and Holy Orders. We wrote to Tom McCabe and other Brooklyn priests. All said the some thing: "Come back to Brooklyn and apply what you have seen in France to the ministry among the poor in Brooklyn." I came back home and told the diocese I needed a year to think about Ordination.

I said, "I'm not sure." Over time I stopped pursuing the priesthood and I took various jobs in the fields of counseling and education. Vatican II said, "The laity is the Church." That was good enough for me.

Then in 1985 Father Francis sent out letters from an old address book to see how many he could reach. It was like putting bottles in the ocean. He did not reach many, but he did reach me. He said he was going to be visiting the Sons of Charity in Montreal in July of 1985 and if anyone received this letter, let him know. He would love to meet us again. I had been thinking about him, wondering if he was still alive. Then when I returned home there was this letter from him. Yet I knew that I would not be in Montreal in July of 1985. I had already tried to get a room in Montreal in July in order to attend a major conference of AA (alcoholics) and Alanon (children of alcoholics) but there was no hotel space available so I had decided not to go. Then at my next regular Alanon meeting it was announced that because of a last minute cancellation there was a room available. I took it or so I thought. When I got to Montreal it turned out that the room was not available, but through another strange circumstance a room right next door was available. I said to myself, "What is going on here? There are over 60,000 people coming to Montreal and I end up with a room without which I never could have come."

I met Father Francis. He came back with me to New York and met John. He asked me what my plans were. I said I was teaching in a Work-Study program in the public schools which meant I was off for the summer. He invited me to France so I went and for three weeks he talked about what he called his "obsession." He said that when he had met me 25 yeas ago he wondered "why" I was thinking about the priesthood. I had so many problems. Now he was wondering "why not?" I was shocked. I had stopped thinking about the priesthood for many years. Francis suggested that there was a team of Sons of Charity

145

in Baltimore and I should go and visit them. Over the next few years I made several visits to Baltimore and worked with the Fils but I could not make the break from Brooklyn. Finally, in January of 1987 I made the break. I quit my job and went to Baltimore and then to Chicago and from Chicago to New Haven, all the time staying with the Sons of Charity and finally, I joined the community.

From the early days, in the '60s when I first met the Sons of Charity, I noticed they had a spirit about them. They seemed to be joyful in being together, in working together. They seemed to be having fun yet they were committed to their ministry. They were putting into practice the "preferential option for the poor" and working people. They were open to all. Now at the tender age of 50, I knew I had to make a decision and I decided. I decided to be a priest and to be a Son of Charity. I had a novitiate year and then, in a formal way, I joined the community. It was quite a journey and I finally stopped running. I was out of breath but filled with the Spirit. A number of people have called it a "Hound of Heaven" story.

I'll go along with that.

I was ordained in 1992, right here in Sacred Heart Church for the Diocese of New Haven. You were here. Bishop Rosazza was the ordaining bishop. It was a great day. I felt the Hound of Heaven had finally caught up with me.

I've been in Sacred Heart since ordination. Right now I feel like I'm doing everything and that's not good. I'm alone in the parish; by "alone" I mean I'm the only priest here. But there are plenty of people in the rectory each day including groups of women who come in and clean and bring supper. Alonzo works here. He's been connected with Sacred Heart for about 10 years. He's married with two girls, one of whom is a Sister with the Apostles of the Sacred Heart which has its Mother House close by. The family is from Colombia and very dedicated to the Church. They see it as a mission.

As a priest I'm alone most of the time. There is one Son of Charity, Fr. Lorenzo, who is 80 years old. He comes down from Canada and spends a month out of every three with me. He is very helpful with getting the parish accounts in order. He is very good at that. I'm glad I have him, if only part-time.

When he is not here, I have all the Masses. But it is not an impossible situation. We have one vigil Mass Saturday evening and two Masses Sunday morning — one in English and one in Spanish.

Then there is the so called "Traditional Latin Mass" at 2 p.m. on Sunday afternoon. We are the designated Church for the whole region. They have priests from outside the parish to say the Mass. Every once in a while they get stuck when the designated priest doesn't show up. They come to me and, if I'm free, I'll celebrate Mass with them, in Latin with my back to the people.

Let's get back to my living situation. I feel it is definitely unhealthy for me and the parish. Everything goes through me. It becomes a burden. Of course, I do relish some quiet time alone. I used to feel obligated to answer every phone call. Now when the phone rings at 9:30 at night, I yell out "I'M CLOSED. LEAVE A MESSAGE AND I'LL CALL YOU IN THE MORNING." If anyone is here in the rectory when I do this, they think I'm losing it. What makes the situation unhealthy for the people in the parish is that they get only one view of things, my view. I miss getting feedback or getting a chance to hear what another person thinks of my ideas.

I don't want to become an "old bachelor" meaning I don't want to become so set in my ways that I am not open to doing things some other way. There is something missing in my way of life here. Also, there is the issue of the rectory.

The rectory is a very large building with three floors and 12 foot ceilings. It has 23 rooms. It was made for four or five priests with each priest having a suite of rooms. It is clearly too big for me. On most nights, I'm the only one sleeping here. Some people will ask me, "Do you live in that big house all by yourself?" Perhaps we could rent out the top floor to some divinity students from Yale which is right down the road from us. Perhaps they could do some work in the parish. We'll have to see. It would be better for me if this residence housed more people. Psychologically, it is not healthy to be alone in such a large house.

I have many parish organizations. Lots of dedicated people involved. But the last time I spoke to them at a general meeting of all the organizations I said to them that our situation reminded me of the Sons of Charity in Montreal.

Twenty-five years ago we had seven priests. Today we have seven priests. The same seven! I asked, "How many of you were with us 10 years ago?" Most raised their hands. I said, "We are all getting old. We need new blood." It was a meeting of all the groups: liturgy, Eucharistic ministers and lectors, teachers, parish council, and faith education (CCD). These groups meet monthly, so for me it means I'm meeting with some group every Wednesday night.

I celebrate Mass in the chapel at 6:15 p.m. and the meeting starts at 7:00 p.m. I'm looking for new leadership, new ideas, new ways to develop people's potential. I try to challenge them. So it is a lot more than just attending a meeting. There are over 100 people involved in some type of ministry. Then there is the Industrial Areas Foundation.

I had known about the Industrial Areas Foundation (IAF) and their philosophy of community organization from the BEC (Brooklyn Ecumenical Cooperative) while I was still in Brooklyn. Then it turned out that an organizer with ties to the IAF was the guest speaker at the first deanery meeting I attended in New Haven.

I got involved from the very beginning with this broad-based community organization which a year later we would call ECCO, which stands for Elm City Congregations Organized, (Elm City is another, earlier name for New Haven).

The first objective of any IAF group is to be recognized. This is done by taking a simple, practical action. Our first action was to show up at the police station with about 80 local residents demanding to see the chief. We had done our homework and had identified those areas in the neighborhood where drugs were bought and sold. But the police chief refused to meet with us. The chief wasn't there (as we expected) but the press was there. We had a "summons" for the chief for not showing up. Gradually we were able to work with the chief and he became an ally.

Our next action was to go after a liquor store that was selling liquor like an open bar a short distance from a school. We closed the place down and we closed down other liquor stores that were operating close to a school. Eventually we passed the "ECCO Law" that no new liquor store could be built within 1500 feet of a school.

Then we went after the proliferation of guns. We are now building houses. We have homes all set for occupancy.

We are starting with six homes. The next stage will be 33 and after that another 60. We use a revolving amount of seed money that we have been able to raise from churches, dioceses and bishops. Each home is individually owned and affordable. The program follows the Nehemiah housing model that has been so successful in Brooklyn and the Bronx.

It comes down to a monthly mortgage payment of about $800 per month. This is what it costs to rent an apartment. But a family who buys one of our homes gets a two-story home with a front and back yard and a basement that can be furnished and rented out. Most of our efforts now are focused on this housing program. It is our major project.

The IAF has a definite philosophy. The issue is not the most important thing. In fact it is the least important aspect. The most important aspect is the work we do on ourselves as leaders. Do I bring people together? How can I improve? The whole purpose of the IAF is to train and develop leaders. It is the same as I am trying to do in the parish, to develop leaders.

There are only four or five priests, including Bishop Rosazza involved in IAF, out of about 16 priests. It's kind of disappointing. It was Rosazza who got the thing started. He brought in the IAF.

Housing is a real problem. Rents are very high. There is a great need for affordable housing. IAF provides the pride of ownership. A family can pay the mortgage with a total income of about $25,000 a year, especially if the family is getting income from a rental.

We try to ground our social actions on a theology. One of our favorite texts is from Exodus where Moses' father-in-law, Jethro, tells Moses he is killing himself by taking care of everyone's problems and not able to do what God has called him to do. Moses agrees and appoints 70 others as leaders to work with the people. This is an important message for all, but especially for pastors. You don't have to do it all yourself. We are in the process of training leaders to take care of many of the problems and concerns of the people.

Time is very important in the IAF. We only have so much of it. We have to respect one another's time and people have to respect my limited amount of time. Meetings must begin on time and end on time. Meetings don't have to last two hours.

On a personal note, I find I am not aggressive enough in asking people to do things and take responsibility for things. I don't like asking others to do what I am not doing and this, I think, holds me back.

Over our chapel in France is a plaque that asks, "How do we combine our pastoral and prayer ministries"? The answer is fairly easy: we should be like Jesus. Very often he was off by himself. No one knew where he was. People were looking for him but he needed his time apart. He was very much a man apart but he also lived with the people.

This goes to the level of worker priests and parish priests. I see the priest as both a man set apart but also one who is immersed in the life of his people. I feel it is both. The Spanish community tends to treat me as one set apart, one who is above them. A priest cannot distance himself so much from his people that he is unapproachable and does not share the feelings and struggles of the people. I feel very needy; for example I need so much more Spanish vocabulary so I can communicate with the Spanish community. I realize the challenges before me. We have in the parish people from more than 16 countries. The Sons of Charity asked the diocese to give us a poor parish. That's the charisma of the community. We take only poor parishes. The particular parish is up to the diocese. They showed us Sacred Heart and that is the parish we took.

I think I got the beginnings of my commitment to the poor from Tom McCabe at St. Ann's parish in Brooklyn. I remember going into poor parishes knocking on doors and taking the parish census. Then I think of my family and the values that came from them.

Certainly the Sons of Charity reinforced this desire to minister to the poor. They helped me also to understand that ministry to the poor is not paternalistic. It is, rather, meeting people where they are and helping them reach their full potential. It is all part of the formation of leaders.

I understand there are not many priests volunteering for inner city work. There is a priest near-by in a parish very much like Sacred Heart with a large Mexican community. He has been very active in ECCO. Now he is retiring and he is not sure anyone will volunteer to take over.

In the past 15 years that I have been in New Haven, I've known of only one priest who asked to work in a poor area. Now some of this is understandable and explainable. Under previous administrations it was commonly thought that the diocese had little regard and respect for the work of the poor parishes. However, under the leadership of Bishop Henry Mansell and Bishop Peter Rosazza poorer parishes receive additional subsidies that are sometimes resented by the richer parishes.

No one wants to see his church or his school or his convent crumbling. But this is what happens and the priest has to go out and beg for money. So many young guys say, "Who needs that? The job is tough enough without that." This, as I said, is understandable. What is not so understandable is that some younger priests seem to be more concerned with their clerical or liturgical attire than with the social Gospel of Jesus Christ. This is what scares me.

In an inner city parish, you know you are going to be alone. There will be no other priest to share the burden. You will not be living with two other priests, as in the "old days." Every phone call, every ring of the door bell eventually comes to you. It's not attractive. It's hard.

Of course it is not only the inner-city. Most of the parishes in the diocese have only one priest. It has become the norm unless you have a real big parish or a special situation. But outside of that, one priest to a parish is the norm around here. We also have the situation where one priest is the pastor of parish A and administrator of parish B. Pretty soon they will be joined. In Hartford three priests are living together and serving four parishes among them.

It is an experiment, but for the most part each priest is on his own. Our training in the seminary was to prepare us to live alone, to do our work and go to our own room. It did not train diocesan priests to live in community. Diocesan priests are not accustomed to work and live together. We do have deanery meetings but I feel more strongly connected to the Spanish deanery meetings that Bishop Rosazza, The Vicar, calls together each month. It is for those priests working in parishes with a large concentration of Latinos.

To tell you the truth I find more connection with the pastors in ECCO which includes women pastors, Lutherans, and Methodists. The meetings with the ECCO pastors are much more fruitful for me than are my own deanery meetings. It is interesting that the collar still means something. Whenever we go on demonstrations the ECCO pastors are reminded to wear the collar because it shows we represent many other people.

We are about 70% Hispanic, still mostly Puerto Rican. In the other 30% we have a small distribution of almost everybody: Haitian, Portuguese, Italian, Irish. Over 16 countries are represented in the parish.

I spoke recently with our new Archbishop, Henry Mansell. I told him that, The Sons of Charity,as such, could not take future responsibility for this parish because we are spread so thin. He called me up. (What a difference from the previous Archbishop!) He said he understood that the Sons of Charity could not keep taking responsibility for Sacred Heart. But in his letter to the community he would ask that I be permitted to stay on as pastor.

Things are pretty much in place. My community would like me to stay considering my age and the work I've been able to do here. It would make no sense for me to have to start all over in a new place. But I did say to the Archbishop that if he wants me to stay there are certain things I will need, such as a deacon. I need help with the administration of the parish.

It's kind of discouraging. The Legionnaires of Christ have a seminary about ten minutes from here. We get their literature – everyone is dressed in cassock. We did that 40 years ago. It's kind of scary.

When I joined the Sons of Charity, I took three vows: poverty, chastity and obedience. Obedience is not a problem because the Community practices an open style of obedience with a lot of consultation. It is not autocratic at all. We don't hear much about poverty. But the three vows are meant to be an ideal for our way of life. They should be a reflection of the lives of our people. Families have to be obedient to life. If a child cries at 2 a.m. parents have to be obedient to that call and get up out of bed to see what the problem is.

There are a lot of people who are celibate today and not by choice. There is the problem of AIDS and that of young adults who would like to marry but cannot find the right person. This puts a great burden on a lot of people. My celibacy is easy. I have it a lot easier than some 25-year-old who's trying to find his or her way in life. I fall in love every day but I don't act on it. I heard about Thomas Merton who fell in love with his nurse, M. Celibacy has not been a great burden to me, probably because I did date women and had a number of relationships before joining the Sons of Charity. Sometimes I miss this desperately, but sometimes I'm just too busy to think about it or feel sorry for myself.

I used to think that we would see the day when priests in community would be celibate and diocesan priests would be married. Now I am not so sure, yet it could be as near as the next conclave. The bishops realize they need help.

Optional celibacy is already being practiced by the married Episcopal and Lutheran ministers who have been ordained to the Catholic priesthood and remain married. One of the priests who comes to celebrate the traditional Latin Mass is married, an Episcopal convert. They had a reception for him and his wife came. I went over to her and said, "You are the first wife of a Roman Catholic priest I have ever met." We need both celibate and married priests. It is not a matter of "either/or" but "both/and." Both can bear great witness. It all depends on how the celibacy or the marriage is lived out.

We had a young fellow who worked here as an intern from Yale Divinity school. It is a shame that he has to choose between marriage and the priesthood. That should not be the choice. The choice should be between being a priest or not being a priest. The second choice should be between marriage or celibacy. Each choice is completely separate from the other.

Besides the vow of chastity, I also have the vow of poverty. I've never been attached to material things. I have enough to live on. I receive a stipend from the community of $300 per month. We have no full-time cook, but the people of the parish bring in meals for me. Some women do it on a regular basis. Alonzo works here as a secretary/pastoral associate. We could use a full-time secretary.

I have a car and a computer. Poverty, like chastity and obedience, is a mirror. There is a great deal of poverty in an area like this and people are struggling. Hopefully my voluntary poverty identifies me with them and their struggles to pay the rent and feed the children. I don't go out much for recreation. I can't remember the last movie I saw. I've taken out membership in a video store and I've gone there on occasion and rented a movie. I think the last one I saw was *Angela's Ashes*.

I don't have a vow "to pray" as I have a vow to be "chaste" but maybe that is not a bad idea. When Fr. Lorenzo is here we try to pray a part of the Office together each day. As a rule, I do not pray the Breviary each day, far from it.

I do try to pray with the people each day. My prayer is centered in the Liturgical life of the parish. I used to offer Mass only on the weekends. Then about two years ago we started a daily Mass at noon during Lent and that has continued. So two or three times a week I celebrate Mass with a small group of parishioners. Then I celebrate Mass on a regular basis at the nursing home. We have an evening Mass followed by Benediction on the First Fridays of the month. For me, the basis of my prayer is the Eucharist with my people.

However I am interested in the Fraternities of Charles de Foucauld for myself. I'd like to know if there is a Fraternity of priests meeting in the New Haven area. If there is, I'd be interested in joining. That would be great.

I make a yearly retreat with the Sons of Charity in Montreal. The last retreat was given by a priest who is a member of a Fraternity of

Charles de Foucauld. I was amazed to see how close the spirituality of the Fraternities is with the spirituality of the Sons of Charity.

The retreat master stressed, for example, the concept of "presence," presence to the working class, presence to the poor. That same idea of "presence" is central to the spirituality of Brother Charles and the Sons of Charity. "Presence" seems to fit right into what we are doing here in New Haven.

I identify with all of this, just as I identified with the retreat master in Montreal. He was invited to give the retreat because of how closely his vision fits into our vision.

I mentioned going on a yearly retreat. The question is, in what other ways do I renew myself? I never was a great reader. I read more off the internet than I read from books. So much comes across my desk that I can't possibly keep up with it. I was reading a lot before the elections. I read right off the screen. What I want to save, I'll print it. We get the *Times* every day but I rarely have the time to read it. I'd like to read Donald Cozzens' book on *The Changing Face of the Priesthood*. I rarely read a book from cover to cover maybe this book will be an exception.

How else do I get renewed? When I let them, the people in the parish renew me. The IAF renews me. The people in the nursing home renew me. Their stories renew me. The pastors in the ECCO group renew me. The priests are discouraged. The new bishop is a breath of fresh air. He appreciates social action. He is grateful for what we do. That renews me.

CHAPTER THIRTEEN

REV. FRANK SHANNON

ONE PRIEST FOR FOUR PARISHES

I was ordained in 1987, incredible! It seems like yesterday.

My first assignment lasted about a year-and-a-half. It was in Astoria, Queens. It had plenty of poor people but the parish was more middle-class than poor. Immigrants were starting to move in. The immigrants were from El Salvador and Honduras and other countries in Central America. Very poor! I started a Spanish Mass in the basement of the Church. And that's where it still is, in the basement of the Church. I said the Mass and it annoyed me that the Spanish Mass was being said in the basement of the Church. I didn't like the way the people were treated. They were not given the respect I thought they deserved. I wanted to bring them up into the main Church but it never worked out. I was too new, too weak to make any real changes so I moved on.

I was assigned right here, to Blessed Sacrament on Euclid Avenue. I was here for about six years. It was a wonderful experience. It was a parish that had everything: Irish and Italian who had been here for many years and now with a massive growth in the Dominican community. Remember, this is now my second assignment to Blessed Sacrament. I have just been reassigned here again. At the end of my first assignment the Spanish population had continued to grow and we had started a second Spanish Mass. Both Masses were packed with 800 to 900 people at each Mass. We also did a lot of evangelization. We went into the neighborhood, rang doorbells, greeted people, and said Mass in front of their houses. I had the help of two Spanish-speaking Vincentian priests. They didn't live here except when they gave the annual Mission. But I was not alone.

John Mahoney was the pastor, a real decent guy. But after more than six years I felt that it was time to move. I knew that Jack Powis was looking for help at St. Barbara's. He was having some health problems. I asked the bishop for a transfer and I went to St. Barbara's. There were just the two of us. I was with Jack for about a year-and-a-half. He took a sabbatical during that time which he could not have done if he were alone. He came back refreshed and they asked me to take a parish in the Bedford Stuyvesant area of Brooklyn. I accepted. I was assigned to be the pastor of two parishes at the same time. At least on paper it was two parishes because the diocese had already doubled up. They had already made two parishes from the original four. St Lucy's had already been combined with St. Patrick's and St. Ambrose had merged with Our Lady of Monserrate. I was covering by myself what used to be four parishes with three or four priests in each parish.

It was quite an experience.

As a matter of fact we are having a meeting this afternoon at the Chancery office with four or five guys who have had experience of being the pastor of more than one parish at the same time. The diocese is trying to get some feedback from us on how things worked out. They want to hear our suggestions and frustrations and there are many.

I'm going to tell them that they are putting together a recipe for burn out. Each of my parishes is big. Each Church has 600 to 700 people on a Sunday morning. Each one has over 200 kids in the CCD program. Each one has baptisms. Each one has funerals. I end up running back and forth between the two places. Each Church has a separate budget and separate Church bulletin. I always felt frazzled. I made a lot of friends and I found many good people, but the administrative work of being the pastor of two inner-city Churches is overwhelming. That's why it is nice to be back here as the pastor of one Church. And even though there are more people in this one parish than there were in the other two parishes combined, it's such a pleasure not to be running back and forth between two parishes on a Sunday morning. It allows me to be more of a pastor.

I took the multi-parish assignment only because I didn't want to see parishes close. That's why I accepted the assignment to be the pastor of more than one parish at the same time, as difficult as that is. I found out quickly that I didn't have any sense of control. I was always wondering what was going on in the "other parish." Each parish wanted me there full time and even though it was unrealistic, each parish expected the same level of service that it had when it had three or four full-time priests in each parish. It was unworkable.

When I told the secretary at Monserrate that I was going to a meeting today on the two parishes and they will be asking for suggestions, she said I should tell them that it was time to "bite the bullet" and close one of the parishes. I said that is exactly what I do not want to happen. She was very kind. She said she realized that I've tried to be with the people and be a pastor rather than an administrator, but it is impossible to be both an administrator and a pastor of two demanding parishes.

The answer, I think, lies in lay leadership. I strongly believe in lay leadership. When I left the parishes to return here to Blessed Sacrament, part of my evaluation was that I had trained leaders to run the parishes. When I first got to the parishes the people expected the priest to do everything and I mean everything from counting the collection to overseeing the accounts of every single group in the parishes. I told the people that if things are going to work then they had to accept more responsibility and I had to put more trust in them. They began to take over such things as wakes and cemetery services. I gave people the keys to the churches and asked them to keep the churches open and be sure they were respected by all. We went to a lot of leadership training. We joined the East Brooklyn Congregations (EBC) and that helped. Some times you have to hear things from outside your local group to realize what has to be done. Business as usual was no longer working. Lay leadership had become essential.

One of the problems with working in the inner city is that often after you have developed leadership the people are ready to move out to a better place and they do. It is like our Catholic schools. We give new teachers two or three years of training and experience and then they get a higher paying job in public school and move on. I don't blame them. They have to eat too. It is just that Catholic schools don't receive the benefit of the training we provide.

Another problem is the lack of community among parish priests. The last deanery meeting was rather depressing. The topic was the closing of 22 Catholic schools in Brooklyn. The only benefit for me was to sit together with all these people and realize I am not alone. We are all in the same boat together. We also meet as members of the EBC. But as far as the Church goes, I do not see much long-term planning going on at either the diocesan level or the grass roots level. A lot of our time goes into meeting the day by day needs of our people which are many. That's just the way things are.

By the way, I guess you know that I became famous a year or so ago when I appeared on the front page of *The New York Times* for December 25, 2004. Personally I came to like the article because for the most part it gave a positive view of the priesthood and we all know there are not many positive articles on priests these days. The picture of me riding a bicycle to visit people in the parish provoked a lot of comment. The article was written by David Gonzales a real friend of priests. I didn't have a chance to read it until I was going home that evening to my grandmother's. I read it as I was waiting for the bus. I thought at first that it was a little negative. He wrote a lot about my work in the parishes but he also wrote about a certain amount of chaos and uncertainty. Most people I've talked to liked it and found it very positive. So I'm pleased about that. I gave him free access to follow me around and see how I spend my time. I was nervous to see how it would come out.

The only reason I said yes to David's request to do a story on me and the two parishes was because he had written such a positive article about Jack Powis' leaving St. Barbara's a few months ago to start a new form of ministry; "A church without walls." David followed me day after day with a photographer taking a ton of pictures. I would say to him, "David, you can get me into a lot of trouble. I could look like an idiot or I could look decent." He saw me in my good moments and in my bad moments. He saw me at Mass and reading in my office. I had to trust him that he would be fair with me and the people, and he was.

I have been asked what influenced my decision to become a parish priest.

Certainly, one influence was, strangely enough, my Catholic elementary school education. Hardly a week went by that the sisters were not collecting for the poor or for the Missions or for some kind of disaster relief. When I entered the seminary, it was not because of some priest but it was because of my seventh grade teacher, a nun. Her commitment to the poor stayed with me. I had Michael Himes in the seminary. He said you have to find your vocation. If you like what you are doing and if the people like you and if you enjoy being a priest then you have found your vocation. I enjoy working with the poor. I have found my vocation.

Out in the seminary, some seminarians made it very clear that they had no interest in working in poor neighborhoods. Some were afraid, afraid that they could be mugged or their car might be stolen. They might be very good men but the inner city was not for them. They were uncomfortable in inner city parishes. They did not even want to come to meetings in inner city parishes.

When I volunteered to work in Bedford-Stuyvesant, I realized that it was not a death sentence. If I found out that this kind of work was not for me I knew I could always request a transfer. But, as a matter of fact, I found that this was the kind of work I loved. I also knew that I had to get out of Astoria because life in the rectory was terrible. So the two things came together and I saw it as Divine Providence in helping me find out what kind of priest I wanted to be.

I took the assignment to go back to Blessed Sacrament because Steve Lynch had volunteered to take my place. Steve is a very good guy. I would not have left Bedford Stuyvesant unless I knew that a person like Steve Lynch was ready to take my place and keep the two parishes open and not be afraid to walk the streets and get into the projects. By the way, Steve is being made administrator, not pastor, of the two parishes because in conscience he could not take the oath pastors have to take. This is a story for another day.

Another factor about being a priest in the inner-city is living alone. It is becoming tougher and tougher to live alone. For the most part I lived alone in St. Patrick's–St. Lucy's because I did not want to leave the rectory vacant. I knew that once the word was on the street that the building was empty, it would be vandalized. Every once in a while I would stay over at Monserrate where a couple of priests were living but working outside the parish. We would have a cup of tea or a glass of wine together and talk about our day, what went wrong and what went right, or about the news. It was a more human way to live. Nothing formal. We did not eat together, but, as I said, it was a more human way to live. I inquired about living in Queen of All Saints rectory which was not too far away but it just didn't work out. Now I'm not one who cries about being lonely. I work hard both day and night. When 11 o'clock comes around I'm exhausted. I'm happy to be alone. But it is nice to have someone in the rectory you can talk to and laugh with, like the six weeks Joe Diele was here before he went to St. Clement's. There were no obligations, no pressures, nothing formal, just another person, a friend to share the day with, a little companionship, a good thing, a good way to live. I see the priest both as a man "set apart" and one who is "immersed in community." For a priest to be effective, he must be both.

I think the people are looking for a leader, a representative of the Church, someone they can go to when in need, someone who is both a friend and a guide, someone who is a little bit different. This is something I struggle with. They want a friend, that is clear to me, but they want something more. They are looking for an instrument of God's graces in a way that they are not going to find it in someone else. The people are not looking for a business man or an administrator. They are looking for a friend and a pastor. Believe it or not, it was the subject of my meditation this morning. So for me it is both. A priest should be one set apart, a man of prayer, the pastor, and a man immersed in his people, a friend.

I also see the priest's role to be both cultic and servant-leader, to develop lay leadership and build the Christian community through Eucharist, prayer and the sacraments. This is the "cultic" part. But also it is important to get out there into the community and meet people and ring doorbells. I call this part of the priest's role as very much the "servant-leader" or simply "getting our hands dirty" part. What concerns me a bit is how younger priests see the priesthood.

I was asked to give a retreat recently to a group of younger priests and they were tough! I tried to get them to be a little more open. I asked them to read the Gospels and see how open Jesus was to people and how he calls us to an openness that was unheard of in his time. I asked them not to be so rigid but to be more flexible. They became a little hostile, a little annoyed with me.

Maybe things are changing. I read that all of the seminarians from Brooklyn and Rockville Centre were invited to spend some time in the Dominican Republic and many went. On the other hand when I met a seminarian from the Archdiocese of New York and told him I had spent some time in the Dominican Republic in order to pick up a little more Spanish, he said, and I quote, "I would not even fly over that place." I'm not sure if he was ever ordained or how many priests he represented, but he was scary.

I think they are still going to close a lot of inner-city parishes unless there is a serious commitment to train lay people and give real responsibility to lay people. If they do this, they will not have to close parishes. But I am afraid that won't happen. Rather than give responsibility to lay people they will close or merge schools and close or merge parishes. People take courses and attend the pastoral institute but are not given the responsibility to run the parish when they are qualified to do so. The diocese will have to either trust some lay people to run parishes or close them.

Where does that leave the ordained priest? I don't know exactly. Priests might end up as "circuit riders" with all sacramental work and little pastoral work. I hope and pray it will not come to that. It would not be good for the people and it certainly would not be good for the priests. I used to hope that things would return to how they used to be with convents full of Sisters and rectories full of priests. Now I know this will not happen. Those days will not come back. I heard just the other day that a convent that used to house 40 Sisters and now had one Sister, finally closed. It is also clear that praying for vocations just doesn't work. The Holy Spirit must be leading us along new paths. But the uncertainties make it hard.

It's interesting for me to come back to a place I had been in nine years ago. We did a lot of work with youth. Now nine years later I am seeing them again. Now they are good young women and good young men. Some are in college. Most have decent work. I can see that seeds that were planted here in youth programs years ago have born fruit. Most priests don't get a chance to see that, so I am blessed. Of course when I was here nine years ago there were four priests and I was able to put a lot of time into basketball and youth programs in general. Now there is only me. I will give as much time as I can to the youth program including taking kids to the beach in the summer time. But I just can't be as visible in these programs as I was nine years ago when there were four of us. I used to be with the kids almost every night.

We need the involvement of the laity. The parish council is a good example of what I am talking about. The previous pastor here at Blessed Sacrament had dissolved the parish council. I've been back here only a month and I'm already starting a parish council. I can truthfully say that during my time in St. Patrick's–St. Lucy's I never did anything without the agreement of the parish council. That's how strongly I believe in lay people taking responsibility for their own church. It is much harder to do it this way than it is doing things alone. But it is better this way.

Years ago Bed-Stuy and Fort Green were the places to be in. There were groups of priests and sisters planning and praying together. It was exciting. Now in these areas there are few priests and almost no sisters. But we must work with what we have – the people. Lay leadership is clearly the way to go. Of course, if some priests or sisters wanted to come in and work with us, they would be most welcome. I have a retired priest who comes in and helps me out from Wednesday to Sunday morning. I don't know what I'd do without him. He speaks a little Spanish, but more importantly, he has a good attitude.

As you know from *The New York Times* article, I travel by bike and public transportation. I don't own a car. The Church building is magnificent but the parish is broke. The rectory is very nice but again we don't have any money. I tell the people that I forgo a lot of luxuries for the good of the parish and I ask the people to do the same. Right now I have my mother's car but it is only to take her to the airport. I like the bike. In a neighborhood like this, it is a good sign and it is actually practical. I've been influenced by St. Francis. I prefer the term "simplicity" to "poverty." I try to live a simple life style.

There is a practical aspect. I save money on parking and repairs. Also, I enjoy riding a bike and the subways are very convenient. So it works for me and it keeps my life simple. It is interesting that once I got rid of my car, I started to do much more reading. Kids think I'm crazy. They reason if you can have something then you should get it. It is counter cultural to them that I could afford a car but I choose not to own one. It makes people think which is what a sign should do. It makes me feel good. It is an example. I don't want to be self righteous about it. That would spoil everything. I do like the reactions I get as I ride my bike in my parish. It makes people take notice and they seem to enjoy watching me and maybe praying for my safety.

I have a story for you. My grandmother, the night before she died, gave me a check for $10,000.00 and said, "Now get off that bicycle and get yourself a car and be respectable." I put the check in the bank and a few days later I said to my grandmother, "You know, I don't want a car. It will just give me ulcers. What I would like is to buy bells for the Church, a chime system." She said, "Well do whatever you want. It is your money now." So I did and that is what is in St. Lucy's now.

I have lost a few bikes, but I have good college friends who stay in touch with me and are very generous to me and to any program I am running. They trust me that I will use their money well and not waste it on myself. I try to live a simple life not because I am heroic but because it fits into my personality and my way of life. I may not get any reward in heaven for being poor but it unclutters my life and gives me room to breathe and be myself. Actually, I probably should not depend on the bike so much and do more walking. I'm not impressed with any priest who drives a big, expensive car. Give me my bike and let me be.

Let's talk about celibacy. It seems to be on everyone's mind so let's talk about it. If I had the option to marry, would I marry? No, I don't think so. As time goes on I'm happy with the way things have turned out. I'm comfortable living a celibate life. I've been celibate for 24 years. I've grown into it. Sure I would not mind once in a while having someone in the bed to turn to. I've never fallen in love with anyone. I have my temptations, but I find my life as a priest all consuming and satisfying.

I was on retreat one time out in Douglaston and the retreat master said, "It is not a question of 'if' you fall in love but 'when' you fall in love and then you have to decide what you are going to do." The fellow sitting next to me said, "Did you hear that, Frank"? I said, "Yes, I know."

I don't question mandatory celibacy much because I don't think it will change for a long time. I would love to see women priests. I would love to see married priests. We seem to be heading in that direction but I don't think we will see a change for a long time.

Married priests would present their own problems, for example, finances. Finances would be an issue for this parish, but it would not be a problem for the people. Not at all. Poor people tend to be very open. They are ready to accept married priests. They couldn't care less if the priest ministering to them was married or celibate. All they want is to have priests who are pastoral.

Married priests might not be the complete answer to the priest shortage but it would help. Most of my friends, all lay people whom I met in college, and all active in the Church, are all open to a married priesthood and the ordination of women. We meet and I bounce many ideas and questions off them. They are my main support group.

Most of my support does not come from fellow priests. I have few priest friends. I talk to these three or four priest friends on a regular basis. I go to priest retreat days and I enjoy them but in terms of quality friendships among priests, I have only three or four.

My whole vocation did not come from priests but from Sister Elizabeth and the other Sisters in my elementary school. My emphasis on simplicity and poverty comes from these Sisters and their life styles.

One of my best friends just left. I met him in O'Neil's one night. We had a couple of beers and I said that I admired the pope. Well, my friend really took exception to that. He said we need change in the Church but it will not happen for generations because this pope has appointed almost all the bishops and he only appoints those who think like him. Optional celibacy will not happen in our lifetime, under John Paul II.

My friend was visibly upset about this. I saw the other day that he has taken a leave of absence. He is a very bright guy. I hope we can remain friends. We are both Ancient Order of Hibernians (AOH) people.

I read, but not a lot. I try to read both religious and secular material. The next book I intend to read is called *The Holy Longing*. I go to confession in St. Francis in the city and the priest asked me what I was reading and I told him I am just finishing *The Adventures of Huckleberry Finn*, and he suggested *The Holy Longing* as had my spiri-

171

tual director. So I figured this had to be a message from God. So that will be the next book I'll read. How could I refuse? I get some support from reading. So I do read, but slowly. I like to know what people are talking about. I read *The Da Vinci Code*.

The priesthood has turned out differently than I expected when I entered the seminary 24 years ago and when I was ordained 18 years ago. I never expected to be alone.

I never thought we would not have nuns working in the parish.

I never thought we might not have a school.

I'm basically happy with the way things have turned out.

I'd like to see more vocations. I'd like to see us keep the school. I have to trust in the Lord that things will turn out all right, that all will be well. I am comfortable with where I am and who I am.

I pray but I always felt guilty about not praying the Office. Now I take it with me on the train and I read as much of the Office as I can.

I meditate each morning, an hour before Mass. I use the form of the Lectio Divina. I'm not trying to present an ideal picture. I am here with my coffee and I devote an hour to be with the Lord in my own way.

At night I walk around and say the rosary. I enjoy the quiet that night brings. I then go into church and sit for a little while in silence.

I find peace. Without this time for prayer I'd give the whole thing up.

I'm trying to enjoy saying Mass and being more reflective during Mass. Some week days at St. Patrick's -St. Lucy's I'd be saying four Masses a day including the funeral Mass.

With the shortage of priests, I realize I will be saying more and more Masses so I had better incorporate the Mass into my spiritual life. I want to not just "say" the Eucharist but "pray" the Eucharist.

CHAPTER FOURTEEN

REV. RICHARD G. SMITH

A NEW GENERATION OF PRIESTS

I'm originally from the Bronx. We moved up to Wappingers Falls near Hopewell Junction when I was eight. I went to Catholic school, St. Columba. I grew up with both my parents and a brother and a sister. Of course my family had a great influence on me. The parish was a diocesan parish but the priests were not very dynamic and did not work much with young people.

Those who had the influence on young people were the Sisters in the school, the Dominican Sisters of Blauvelt. Sister Maria Assunta was especially good to me. She was important because she introduced me to the Dominic Savio Club run by the Salesians. I joined the club and the Salesians had a great influence on me, more than the parish priests did. For a while I thought of becoming a Salesian. I spent a year with them, the year between College Seminary for the Archdiocese of New York and the Major Seminary.

I was sure when I left the Archdiocese that I was doing the right thing. But when I got to the Salesians, even though I met some great men who were doing wonderful work with youth and I enjoyed working with them, I came to the conclusion that this was not for me. So after spending a year with the Salesians, I returned to the Archdiocese and entered the Major Seminary to begin the study of Theology at Dunwoodie in Yonkers.

For me the seminary was a mixed bag. There were some things there that were very good. The Liturgy was done well. It was a good model. There was a great library, one of the finest Theological libraries in the country.

The number of applicants was still going up. When I graduated from the College Seminary, they had to build an extension because the number of students was increasing. There were about 60 people living there in my time.

At the very end of my seminary training, numbers started to decline but nothing like the small numbers we have today. I should add that the three years I spent in the College Seminary were among the happiest three years of my life. We had real community, some wonderful professors and although we were being evaluated, evaluation did not consume the place.

Now there are about 30 seminarians for New York, spread out over four years, not many. There were some good things about Dunwoodie. I made great friends there and I appreciate that. On the other hand the faculty created a very suspicious environment. It was a very hostile place. There were some very good professors, two or three whom I admired a lot. But for the most part the faculty worked against the development of community. They tore down trust between students. These were actually the worst four years of my life.

As I said, the seminary was a mixed bag. I did not get a great education but in some areas I got a good education. A lot depended on what you wanted to do and how much time you were willing to put in. There was an education to be had there if you wanted to go out and get it.

There were some great priests on the faculty. So there were some things I really liked about the seminary and some things I actually miss. But I would not want to go back. If I had known what those four years were going to be like I would not have gone to Dunwoodie. Of course, some things are just part of seminary life, the constant evaluations for example, also the voting on you at the end of each year.

Was I prepared for the priesthood when I left the seminary? Maybe no seminary can prepare you for the reality of the priesthood. The pastoral program was a good preparation. Much of the Theological disputes we had in the seminary are pretty far removed from what goes on in a parish. Life in a seminary is a very bizarre, rarified life. You are removed from real life and you're treated as if you have no idea what life is all about.

On the other hand we had some wonderful teachers. Bob Imbelli stands out. He taught a very influential course on Ecclesiology. He preached at my first Mass and I'm still friendly with him. John Quinn was a great teacher of Dogmatic Theology. He is retired now. Tom Shelley was also a great teacher. He taught History and is now at Fordham. They were a group of men who prepared themselves intellectually and spiritually to teach in the seminary. They tried to prepare us for the priesthood, as much as they could.

We had a faculty member who was a very good teacher. I learned a lot from his classes. But he was unfriendly. He was suspicious but not a bad teacher. He's been teaching at the Seminary for a long time, very competent, but suspicious and he was not the only one.

Their way of acting was that they belonged to a club, a boys' club called the priesthood and we, the seminarians, wanted to join that club. Their job was to find out as much as they could about us, evaluate us frequently and see if we were worthy of admittance into their club. I managed to jump over enough of their hurdles and was ordained in 1997, about nine years ago.

During these nine years in St. Peter's in Haverstraw I've spent a lot of time and energy on youth ministry trying to develop a comprehensive program and not just a club that meets once a week. I'm proud of the youth ministry. I think it is a good program. Over the past few years I've stepped back a bit to let the lay leadership have more and more responsibility. I think the total youth program has a good foundation.

I also have some regrets with the youth ministry. When I started the youth ministry, my intentions were to have one program for the entire parish: Spanish-speaking and English-speaking. Now nine years later I have not been able to bring them together under the umbrella of God's TYM (Total Youth Ministry).

There remains a Spanish youth group in the parish that is very divisive. The reality is that all the youth in the parish are Hispanic so there is a very false and unnecessary division between the two groups. So I regret that I have not been able to change that and when I leave St.

Peter's the division will still be there.

I also regret that I did not make the time to be involved in more community events. There is a value to be seen as one who gives time to the entire community and not just to the smaller Catholic community. For example, I've been asked to be the chaplain for some community groups and I've turned them down due to lack of time. I could have been more involved in People to People, a breakfast program right here in St. Peter's basement. All these community programs give you a chance to meet people you can not meet through Church. As a newly ordained priest I made numerous mistakes that I am still living with. My next assignment will give me a chance to make other mistakes, not the same mistakes I made in St. Peter's. I realize now the value of community involvement in a way I didn't realize nine years ago.

There is one thing I was not prepared for and that is that the priest is such a public figure. I find that very hard. Being a public figure is the hardest part of the priesthood for me. I remember the first time I was in the parking lot dressed in regular clothing and some one said, "Hello" to me. "How are you doing, father?" I had no idea who that person was. It just struck me that I have no privacy. If I go into a store to buy something, people hear about it. I was not prepared to have such a public life and for me that is very difficult. I am more of a private person. I did not realize what a public figure I was until I began living the life of a priest. There is no way of knowing what it means to be a public person until you experience it. Even the way the rectory here is set up, there is not much privacy. I try to protect whatever privacy I can.

St. Peter's is a pretty traditional parish in its structure and its congregation. My ministry here for the past nine years has been a pretty traditional priestly ministry. So for me the shocker, the unexpected, has been the lack of privacy.

I take preaching seriously. It is an important part of my ministry. I put a lot of time into it. People have a right to expect a well prepared sermon. I make a lot of notes I find that if I don't have notes. I ramble. But I'd like to get away from the notes, leave them on the pulpit and preach from the middle aisle where, I think, I am more engaged with the people. So there is some tension for me about the use of notes. Most of the time I stay at the pulpit and use the notes.

Being ordained less than ten years puts me in the category of being a "young" priest. I hear a lot of comments about "the next generation of priests," about how we dress and what assignments we are willing to accept. The problem with making these distinctions is that they label people and put them into little boxes. I know individual priests around my age or younger who are reactionary while others border on the radical. The same can be said of older priests. Some of the worst reactionaries I know are in their 70's. I have spent my nine years in the priesthood with priests who are in the older age group and I have respected and loved these older priests.

On the other hand my closest friends are priests around my age group and there is a wide variety of opinion and ways of thinking among them. I am aware that the Hogue study isn't the only study to label younger priests as more conservative than older priests. So there is probably some truth there, but within both groups there is a wide variety of opinion on issues in the Church and in the world. That's been my experience. Of course remember that New York is a fairly conservative diocese to begin with.

The priests who have a reputation for being social activists in the Archdiocese of New York got into this ministry fairly early in their priesthood and stayed in it. They are certainly in the "older" group. I am not aware that they ever seriously tried to communicate their ideas and vision of priesthood to others. I'm not saying this to fault them but merely to say that it never happened. There are a number of priests in the South Bronx who are still considered social activists today. But, as I said, I am not aware of any attempt on their part to communicate a different vision of Church or priesthood.

One problem with younger priests going into inner-city work is the huge language differences that we were not prepared for in the seminary. Most of the young priests do not know Spanish. Of course the Archdiocese could see to it that priests learn Spanish before being sent to a parish where the dominant language is Spanish. Also, you'd be alone in just about every inner city parish. Priests are notorious for their lack of fellowship and reaching out to each other. So a young priest going into an inner city parish would be very much alone and may not know the dominant language of his people. There are a lot of factors that make inner city ministry unattractive. There is more to it than just lack of zeal.

It is becoming the norm that each parish has only one assigned priest. In fact I expect that the only time in my priesthood when I would not be living alone are these years here in St. Peter's. I fully expect that this will be the last time I will be living with another priest. In my next assignment I expect to be alone. One of my best friends is a priest living and working in Harlem. He is in a very poor parish. He replaced a priest who had been an activist 30 years ago. He is alone.

It is easy to blame younger priests. But I wonder why, if the vision of the priest as a change agent in society was so strong, why did it never catch on? Where are all the disciples? For me, the bottom line is that younger priests, like older priests, will go where they are sent. This is also my attitude. I will go wherever I am sent, be it the South Bronx or Westchester County. I will go to wherever I am sent.

This conversation about different attitudes or different ways of thinking among priests touches on a serious problem in this diocese, namely, the lack of priestly fraternity. We don't reach out to help one another. At a recent priest meeting the priests gathered asked the question, "When will we meet again?" but I asked the question, "Who are we? Are we a we?" I don't think so. We are very divided.

I don't think our division comes from ideology. There are ideological differences certainly. I think our divisions are rooted in fear. Priests are happy in their own little world and in their own parishes. Things are functioning fairly well. There is security. There is no need to worry about anything else. There is a lot of fear in the priesthood, fear of change, fear of being labeled "disloyal." Fear is crippling. Our divisions, as I see them, do not come from ideological differences but come from fear.

A priest is very dependent on his bishop and on the chancery office. As priests get older they realize more and more that their pensions and health benefits come from the bishop and his office. There is therefore a reluctance to criticize the bishop publicly or criticize publicly how the diocese is run.

The older you get the more you are dependent on the diocese to take care of you. Like everyone else, the priest has to be concerned about his pension and health benefits. And the older he gets the more he becomes dependent on the diocese to take care of him, especially if he becomes sick. With this dependence comes the fear of speaking out against the "hand that might some day be feeding him."

There is also the factor that we not only want to please other priests and be considered members of the priestly fraternity in New York, but most especially we want to please our father, the Archbishop of New York. We all want to be his favorite and even compete with others to be his favorite and be an "insider" in the diocese. I think this is where the problems in the priesthood in the Archdiocese are rooted: not in ideas but in fear, fear of all the things we have been talking about. It is this fear that is crippling us, fear of being labeled a "trouble maker," fear of being labeled "disloyal" to the Archbishop and the diocese. These are powerful psychological factors especially for men who are celibate and dependent on their peers for emotional support in hard times. There is no wife or family to turn to.

Clerics can be not only non-supportive but catty and gossipy at times. No one wants to be the butt of this gossip. There is no place to hide, so as a result no one wants to "put himself out there." It is easier to be part of the crowd, the good guys.

I want to finish off what I was saying about inner-city work. It is tough work. It was always tough work but it has gotten harder. I'm talking about Spanish-speaking parishes in the inner city. There are a lot of parishes with priests who have come from outside the diocese. Communication can be difficult.

Many people want priests from their own country and culture to be their priest. So in parishes that are heavily Dominican, many of the people prefer a Dominican priest. It can be a problem. I don't hear the optimism for "Spanish work" as I understand there was in the 50's and 60's. Without that optimism it is easy to get worn down and discouraged.

My basic point is that priests will go where they are told to go. A friend of mine did volunteer for inner-city work. He went down to Bolivia to study Spanish and now is a pastor in the Bronx. So he volunteered and he would be considered a "younger priest," just two years older than I am. He volunteered. Others can be assigned.

My thought is that we have to look at individuals rather than groups because it is individuals, not groups, who want to work or who don't want to work in the inner city. It is individuals, not groups, who are reactionary or who are progressive.

We recently had a very discouraging incident. Here was a well known New York priest, Msgr. Harry Byrne, being very critical, in public, of "younger" New York priests. He said that younger New York priests are more concerned about the length of their surplice and the size of their French Cuffs than the needs of the poor. It came out right around the time of the sexual abuse scandals. *The New York Times* carried Burns' remarks on the front page. It was very disheartening because he is being very critical of younger priests without knowing any younger priests.

When I entered the Salesians, I must have gotten 20 or 30 letters welcoming me into the community. When I became a priest of the Archdiocese I did not receive any letters welcoming me into the fraternity of priests in New York, I was not even welcomed into the local Vicariate of Rockland County as a newly ordained.

There is absolutely no outreach among New York priests. Harry Byrne does not know a single younger priest. He shouldn't be considered an expert on a subject of which he had no experience and therefore a subject he just doesn't know, except what he has heard at cocktail parties. To think of oneself as an expert on many issues is endemic to the priesthood. As a matter of fact we are experts of a very narrow field.

Byrne's remarks were unkind, uncharitable, against priestly fraternity and untrue because he had no experience to base his remarks on. He divided; did not bring people together and passed judgment and hurt people he did not even know. Byrne's comments underline the problems of the New York priesthood in general. We do not reach out to one another. No one has ever asked me how my priesthood is going. No one has ever asked me if things are ok. Not once in nine years. It blows my mind. It seems to me that some one in the diocese should care how I'm doing. It boggles the mind that no one seems to care.

A classmate of mine has already left. No one reached out to him. No one reaches out to anyone. Everyone is busy and under a lot of stress but it seems to me that it should be some one's job to reach out to priests.

I was left here alone for two-and-a-half months between pastors and no one ever called to see how I was doing. No one called to tell me that Fr. Madden had been appointed here as pastor. I had to hear it as a rumor. It was no way to treat a newly ordained priest completely inexperienced in administration. As I said, during the two-and-a-half months when I was the administrator of the parish, I did not receive one telephone call asking how I was doing and did I need help. It boggles the mind. If the Church was the local Mac Donald's franchise, it would be closed and out of business. Of course, we shouldn't have to wait for diocesan structures. We should be reaching out to each other on our own.

Many priests are over burdened with work in the parish and don't have time for issues outside the parish, no matter how worthwhile. Also people get very comfortable in their own world, with their own routines. Change is difficult.

Vatican II is one of the issues where there is a real division by age. Remember Vatican II is an historical event for younger priests. It was over five years before I was born. I look at it much differently than someone who was living at the time of the Council.

My generation of priests certainly studied the decrees of the Council but that is not the same as someone who lived through and followed the debates and the shifts made by the Council. There was an enthusiasm at that time, I am told, that cannot be duplicated 40 years later.

If there is a division between older and younger priests, and in this case I think there is, the division is in the interpretation and implementation of the decrees of Vatican II. There certainly are those who feel that the authentic interpretation of Vatican II is the interpretation of John Paul II.

The only Church I know is the Vatican II Church. I never heard Latin at Mass for example, until I entered the seminary. Most of my teachers in Catholic school were lay people. I don't hear people saying that the Council went too far. Rather it is accepted as an historical fact and, as I said, the Vatican II Church is the only Church we know. There is a call for Vatican III and the call comes from both sides, either to continue the reforms of Vatican II or to rein in the "excesses" of Vatican II.

The funeral Mass for John Paul II can be looked upon as a testimony to the reforms of Vatican II. The Mass was held outdoors facing the people. It was an ecumenical service with people from various religions participating. The first reading was done by a woman. Much of this would have been inconceivable before Vatican II. Now we take it for granted, forgetting where it came from.

Statements from the Vatican on the interpretation of Vatican II tend to come from people who are not in pastoral ministry and are not in parish life. The laity has taken ownership of certain ministries, such as Eucharistic minister, and you can't just take them away. It is a good ownership. Many of these statements are just politely ignored or not put into practice.

These statements might come from fear or a concern about the erosion of the role of the priest. From my point of view, I am extremely grateful that there are people who are willing to come here on a Sunday morning and take on different forms of ministry.

It makes no sense to me that one could be a servant of the people and not have any involvement in worship. Nor can there be authentic Liturgy unless we are involved in people's lives and issues of peace and justice.

The models of priest as either cultic leader or servant leader are meant to be integrated. I think Harry Burns would describe younger priests as more "cultic minded" and older priests as more "servant minded." Truth lies in the integration of these two models.

To tell you the truth I don't know what these distinctions really mean. I do know that for me the Liturgy is extremely important and if it were not for the Liturgy I would not be a priest. But Liturgy is not all there is to priestly ministry. Hopefully what we do on Sunday has some carry over to how people live during the week and the Sunday homily has meaning as to how people choose to live their lives during the week.

Serving people includes celebrating Eucharist with them, baptizing their children, marrying them, visiting them when they are sick, and teaching them. All of these are ways of serving people. We need both to be authentic. We both serve the needs of people and we celebrate Eucharist and sacraments with them.

I never took a vow of poverty so my call to poverty is the same as any Christian's. A New York priest does not have a large salary so unless one has money from family or some other source, a New York priest is going to have a pretty simple lifestyle and this is how it should be.

As parish priests there are certain things we need. We need a car. We need a computer. I don't own a lot of material things. I bought my first new car recently and one of the kids said, "you're living the life." It bothered me that he would think that I'm living the life. I don't think I'm living an affluent life style. I own very little. Most of what I own are books. It's important for priests to live a simple life style, as it is for any Christian.

I know I don't have any money. As I said, I recently bought a new car but this was the first new car I ever had and I had to save money over eight years in order to buy it and make the payments. As far as material things go, that's it! Poverty is a value not only for priests but for all Christians. We cannot serve both God and money.

There is something distasteful for me when I do see a priest obviously living a high life style, like driving a very expensive car. On the other hand, it drives me nuts when a priest dresses like a slob. I don't think living a simple life means you dress like a slob or like a bachelor. For me personally I hope to lead a simple life and in this to answer the call of Jesus which is the call of all Christians to love Jesus and not the pleasures that material things promise to give us.

Let's talk about marriage and celibacy. Marriage is a relationship and relationships mature us. There are things we learn in relationships that can not be learned outside of a relationship. Relationships call us to do things that we would not do if left to ourselves. There is a selfishness among some priests and a self-centeredness among some priests that might come from not being in a relationship but living the life of a bachelor who has his routines that no one can change. There is a lot of that.

If you had asked me if I would have chosen marriage if optional celibacy had been available at the time of my ordination, I would have found it difficult to answer. I don't think you are called to marriage in some vague, general sense. You are called to love and cherish a particular person. If marriage had been a choice for me but I had not met the particular person whom I loved and who loved me, I would have chosen celibacy. Both celibacy and marriage are personal choices and it is a mistake to mandate either one.

What bothers me about the whole optional celibacy thing and with women's ordination is the ban on discussion. How does it hurt to discuss it and to listen to people's different experiences? I see major problems in the Church with a mandated celibate priesthood and many men living without healthy relationships or forming hurtful relationships. But I also see problems with the Church supporting married priests. I think there is a lot to talk about but if you don't talk about it what happens? Nothing happens or people go off and do "their own thing." I don't have an agenda here but it bothers me that we cannot openly and honestly discuss things.

There is no harm done by discussing the issues of optional celibacy and the ordination of women. We must create the atmosphere where priests can speak openly and candidly about their experiences as a celibate man and women can speak openly and candidly about their experience. How does it hurt to listen to each other? I don't know what the answers are but at least we should be talking to each other and without fear.

I am thinking of a classmate of mine who left. He was desperately lonely. The priesthood can be a very lonely life but so can marriage.

The priests who left in my time have all left to get married.

The thing that has shocked me most as a priest is to find out how many people are unhappy and lonely in their marriages. It has shocked me. Absolutely shocked me! It is a crisis in the Church that we hardly acknowledge. It is discouraging to me. A lot of it is because of selfishness on the part of one or both or they never really thought of their relationship beyond the wedding day.

More and more you see priests living alone in rectories that were built to comfortably house four or five priests. It is a very difficult thing and depressing. There is a great lack of accountability in living alone. Not only is there no one to share with but there is no one to hold you accountable. There are no checks. It is easy to take up drinking because there are no checks, no one to give you feedback, no one to see you. That is not good. A priest could be suffering from mental illness and there is no one to say, "You need help," or a priest is drinking too much and there is no one to say, "your drinking is out of control."

Sexual abuse by priests has had an effect on me and on most priests. It has made me more cautious. Seminary training was careful to prepare us to relate appropriately to young people. But even with that, combined with the training I received from the Salesians, I am more cautious today than I had been. I sometimes wonder what people think of me. Do they think of me as a child molester even though they don't know me?

But the bigger thing for me has been a great disillusionment with the institutional Church, the bishops. And they still don't get it. This disillusionment with the Church has had a great impact on me and that won't change. I had thought the Church was better than that.

The family bond between bishop as father and the priest as son has been broken. Now the only relationship with the bishop is a legal relationship, not a father-to-son relationship. The bishops made it clear at their meeting in Dallas, Texas, that their first priority was to protect themselves.

The Dallas Charter betrayed priests and so now we can't trust our bishops to have our best interests at heart. It will be very difficult for the bishops to regain the trust we once had in them.

On the other hand, it has purified the motive to become a priest. No one would become a priest these days because of a priest's standing in the community or because of the respect a priest receives. This is a good thing. It has brought about a certain amount of purging. For a young man to become a priest today, he must really want to be a priest. This is an example of some good coming out of evil.

My own support comes from friends. I have good friends in the priesthood.

At this point I do not really have strong lay friends. Lay friendships suffer when you move to the seminary. I have family, close family ties. I have lay friends but not strong lay friends.

My best friends are classmates or those ordained around my time. We talk. We go out. The two pastors I've been with are exceptional priests. They are good friends to me.

I find it sad that many priests do not have good priest friends. I was lucky. I made good friends in the seminary. It is one of the things I am grateful to Dunwoodie for. To have friends you have to work at it. It makes me sad to see some priests so disconnected. On a day off they might spend it walking around the mall. Actually I'd like to have a wider circle of friends. But it is hard to find the time.

Also, I've found it hard to build strong friendships with people in the parish. There seems to be a barrier there even though I am friendly with many parishioners and I'd like to stay in touch with them for the rest of my life. I haven't figured it out yet.

I read a lot of poetry and I read books about art. Poetry and art are my major interests outside of Theology. Poetry is important to me. It makes me look at the world differently. John Paul II wrote poetry and Ratzinger wrote the introduction to the Pope's latest book of poems. It is interesting to note that the Pope is a published poet and the Archbishop of Canterbury is also a published poet.

My life is hectic with my parish duties plus my course work at Fordham in pursuit of a doctorate in Theology with an emphasis on the writings of the early Church Fathers. One of the good things about my formation in Dunwoodie was the insistence on the importance of the Divine Office for the spiritual life of the priest. It is filled with poetry, the Psalms. There are readings from the Fathers of the Church.

As a Deacon I made the promise to read the Office every day. I do well with organization and structure. An obligation is good for me. Then there is the daily celebration of Mass.

I wish I could say that I consistently make a Holy Hour each day but I don't. When I do make time for a Holy Hour, my life is much richer. I do make a yearly retreat in a hermitage and these retreats have become the center of my spiritual life. It is very easy not to pray.

My life as a priest is not much different than the life of a Christian. Most people would be surprised to hear that. They think a priest spends the whole day at prayer. I have to make time for prayer just as a lay person has to make time for prayer. My prayer life centers around the daily reading of the Office, daily Mass and the yearly retreat in the hermitage.

My Theological studies are a kind of prayer for me. Francis de Sales said, "For a priest, the eighth sacrament is study." My studies make me read the Fathers and the Scriptures more closely and more prayerfully.

I enjoy being a priest and being a priest in this parish and in New York, even though we have our problems. I hope this comes across.

Hidden Holiness: Voices of Priests

CHAPTER FIFTEEN

REV. ROBERT VITAGLIONE

IMMIGRATION PRIEST

I was ordained for the Diocese of Brooklyn in 1976, and I've been here in St. Joseph's since 1983. Before coming to St. Joseph's, I was in Our Lady of Loretto in East New York for four or five years. I was in Transfiguration in Williamsburg for a short time both as a deacon and as a priest but it was a very significant time for me. I met one of our "giants," Bryan Karvelis, and I learned Spanish.

I realize I have the reputation of being a lawyer but I am not a lawyer. I never took the bar exam.

The Attorney General of the United States accredits certain non-lawyers to practice "immigration law." They have been doing this for over 80 years. I received training from people at the US Catholic Conference. I applied for and received accreditation as one who has a certain expertise in immigration law. That's how the rumor started that I am a practicing attorney. However I am an immigration lawyer and I do spend a lot of time each day in the courts.

Very often I do spend the morning and afternoon hours in Immigration Court. Then I'm back here at night for parish work, especially helping immigrant parents understand and deal with the behaviors of their teenage children. Not easy! On other days I might spend just the morning or afternoon at the court. It all depends on the court schedule for that day.

We have an Immigration Office in the parish where people can talk to someone about their immigration problems. The immigration office is also open to people who come with regular parish concerns such as a pregnant teenage girl and I deal with that.

In the immigration office I have a team of lawyers who volunteer their time. I also have a few who are paid on a part-time basis. Then there is a whole slew of passionate volunteers, many of whom we saved from being deported. They will do anything for me. They are grateful to me for keeping them here, for keeping spouses here, for helping find loved ones.

I have been able to save thousands of people from being unjustly deported.

Most of them faced deportation either for petty crimes or for crimes they did not commit. Undocumented immigrants, charged with a crime, are the true outcasts of our society. They are like the lepers of Jesus' time. I see St. Joseph's as the modern Island of Molokai, the refuge for lepers. I guess that would make me a modern Father Damien. It could be a lot worse.

As far as my own priesthood is concerned I follow the lead of Msgr. Jim Coffey. I am first of all a man and I will always remain a man. Then through Baptism I am a Christian, a disciple of Jesus. Then I became a priest, one called to preside over a community of believers. I do not bring the faith to the people. The faith is already there. I hope to nourish, develop and celebrate that faith that was here before I ever came on the scene. It is in finding their faith that I find my own and I have found great faith among the people. Tremendous faith.

I believe in the Holy Spirit. I believe the Holy Spirit is guiding the Church and this parish and my work. I have found holy people in each of the parishes where I have worked. I turn to them for advice and for prayer for those who are in need of prayer. I have found many lay people who are close to God. They are the saints of this world, saints with a small "s". They are an important part of the "communion of saints."

We have a large plant here at St. Joseph's, big rectory, big church, big convent, big school, extensive grounds. The parish buildings take up almost a full city block.

The main church seats 2,000 people and another 2,000 people could be accommodated in the lower level church. It is certainly one of the largest churches in the Diocese of Brooklyn.

All the pews have been removed from what used to be the lower level church. It can now hold over 1,000 people with tables and chairs for a dance or a social gathering. In the old days here they would fill both the main church and the lower level church for Masses on Sunday. It must have been quite a sight! This is where many Irish and Italian politicians would come to Mass on Sunday, if only to be seen.

Now about 300 to 400 people come to Mass on Sunday. At the English Mass we get a little over 100 people. At the Spanish Mass we get from 200 to 300 people depending on the weather or time of the year.

I say Mass in English, Spanish or French. I give the homily only once and I use the dominant language of the group that has gathered for Mass. It is usually in Spanish. But I include all three languages in the prayers of the Mass.

I never went to Language School. My only Language School was Father Bryan Karvelis and the time I spent with him in Transfiguration parish as a deacon before ordination and as a priest after ordination. I went to Transfiguration speaking only a few words in Spanish and came out a year later fluent in Spanish. My Italian background helped a lot.

To get back to my situation in St. Joseph's, the school was closed about seven years before I got here. It is now used by Catholic Charities as an SRO (Single Room Occupancy) for senior citizens. The school classrooms were converted into small apartments for those 65 years and older who can basically take care of themselves. They do not need assisted living.

The convent is in a period of transition. It used to be a residence under the control of the Archdiocese of New York for Persons In Need of Supervision (PINS). That closed and the Franciscan sisters came in and set up a substance abuse center. The sisters also moved out and the program was closed.

The school might become a branch of Brooklyn Law School. Several of the lawyers who work for me want to set up a training program on immigration law. It would provide some much needed revenue for the parish.

My main concern is that the building be used in some constructive way. I hate to see it unoccupied.

There is a very large area next to what used to be the convent. It was a garden for the Sisters who taught in the school. But after the sisters moved out many years ago it, had become a garbage heap. The priests who were here didn't bother with it. In the early 90's I, along with a group of parishioners, cleaned it up. It is huge, about 100 by 100. We use it for our sports program. We have a volleyball league and a baseball league that use the area. That's how big it is. It is a Little League field.

Now I'm talking about little kids, not Yankee Stadium. We have our own league with four teams. We had games just last Sunday. It's a lot of fun. I enjoy watching both the baseball and the volleyball games.

I believe in sports as essential to a parish. It builds cooperation and teamwork which are so important. Kids need the chance to work together.

Teaching religion is not enough. Sports give me access to many people. The volleyball league is not for children but for young adults. It is taken seriously. We give out trophies at the end of the season.

I try to keep the buildings in good shape but I am limited by my budget. Let me give you an example.

Our stained glass windows are beautiful but several of them had to be removed because they were in danger of collapsing. So we have four or five empty spaces where there used to be windows. The windows are being saved as we wait for the money to repair them. But right now we do not have the money and the repairing of stained glass windows is very expensive.

I'm fortunate that my Dad was a very handy guy. He taught me plumbing, electricity, boiler repair, etc. Over the years I've fixed the boiler myself several times. If I can't fix the problem, then I will call in a professional, but most of the time I can make the repairs myself and save a great deal of money.

I don't want to present a very bleak picture for St. Joseph's or the Church. I'm not worried about the future because the Holy Spirit will provide. Not to trust in the Holy Spirit is a sin, right?

I'm not in any kind of panic about the future of the Church. It will last until the end of time. But the Holy Spirit might bring new structures that we cannot predict right now. We may see a sister or a deacon or a lay person running the parish when I am gone and there is no priest to take my place. The Holy Spirit always provides but sometimes in ways we do not expect.

I see the future of the Church to be in lay leadership. I spend a great deal of time training lay leaders.

I don't send people to any kind of leadership training programs although these programs can be valuable. The people learn leadership by working with me. That's the kind of training I'm talking about.

Right now we are getting a Bible Study class started. It is for our young people. I run it once a week along with Sr. Julie who works full time in the parish but doesn't live here.

Four people live in the rectory. Sr. Geraldine lives here. She and Sr. Julie belong to a Nigerian order called Daughters of the Divine Love. Julie works here full time but lives at St. Teresa's with other sisters from her congregation. Geraldine teaches in the elementary school in Queen of All Saints and does some parish work here for us.

We don't have a secretary or a cook. We cook for ourselves. We have two women who were burned out of their homes years ago. They live here and one night a week they cook for me. And, of course, I live here. There are four in a rectory that used to house 12 priests. We have a lot of empty rooms. On an emergency basis, people have stayed in the rectory for short periods of time.

Of the 12 priests who lived here, eight worked in the parish including the pastor, the famous Dr. Edward Lodge Curran who never let you forget he had his Ph.D.

Two priests lived here but taught in the Minor Seminary which was only a few blocks away. Another two also lived here but worked in the Chancery Office which was also only a few blocks away. It must have been quite an operation!

Eight priests worked in the parish and now there is only one. We use the dining room for weekday Mass. If we had to, we could seat at least 100 people in the dining room. That's how big the place is and each priest who lived here had his own suite of rooms

I lead a pretty simple life. That's how I think it is supposed to be. For me, poverty means relying on the Holy Spirit, not on material things. For me, poverty is an extension of the Incarnation.

My people are poor. For me, to be identified with them I must be poor. My life must be simple. I learned this from priests like John Powis and Bryan Karvelis and my great uncle who was an order priest and took a vow of poverty. They were my mentors in the spiritual life. I consider myself poor.

I own a car. It is 20 years old, a 1984 Buick with 45,000 miles on it. I live on the subways. They are the life blood of our city. They are my primary means of transportation. I would be embarrassed to have a luxury car while my people are walking or taking the subway.

Celibacy has worked for me. I don't think I could be a good husband to a woman with all the craziness I have in my life. With all my running around, I wouldn't be able to give her the time she deserves.

I do miss not having children. But I realize that if I had my own children, I wouldn't be able to give as much time to the children here as I do. I do have nephews and great nephews. In my sister's parish in upstate New York they had a married Catholic priest who was a convert from the Episcopal Church. My sister said it worked out fine. He was recently transferred to the Bronx.

The mistake we have made is that we have tried to legislate a charism. You can't legislate a charism. We've tried to negotiate with God. You can't do that.

You can't make it a requirement for the priesthood like saying that all those who want to be priests must be at least five feet 10 inches or more. It would be absurd to have such a physical requirement for the priesthood. But even if you had a physical requirement for the priesthood, celibacy is a gift not a physical requirement.

To make it a requirement for the priesthood is to miss the point. We don't rely enough on the Holy Spirit. We are all children of Adam and we try to bargain with God instead of relying on God.

For me, celibacy works out better but I know others for whom marriage and priesthood would have worked out fine. I'm thinking of people like John Mulhern. It is a shame that he could not remain an active priest after he married. Karvelis supported him.

I'm a great sports fan. Sports renew me. If the Yankees are in town, you will find me up at the Stadium. It is my home away from home. In the winter time I'll be at Madison Square Garden if the Rangers are in town.

I have some connections and usually I can get tickets. But I have more connections with the Devils than with the Rangers. That's how I got my picture taken with the Stanley Cup. The Devils have good programs for young hockey players. Hockey is one of my passions. I am so pleased that the young people here have an interest in floor hockey. Hockey is so foreign to Latin American and city youth that I was afraid it would not go over. But we play floor hockey in the basement and they love it.

I love to see girls playing with such passion. It teaches them teamwork. It teaches them values like protecting one another. It is a great game for both boys and girls.

I don't have many priest friends. This work here is so consuming that I don't have much time to go out and meet other priests. The people of the parish are my friends.

I don't see any distinction between a parishioner and a friend. I get support from the people here. They love me and I love them. I don't have to look outside the parish for support. I find support right here. I hear from the Vicars about having priest friends and I don't buy it. I am a man first, not a priest first and I get plenty of support from the people I serve.

I don't believe that my best friends should be priests as if the people are not good enough to be my friends. Jimmy Breslin mentions this in his book, *The Church that Forgot Christ*. He says priests think they have to stick together because they feel they are under attack. I don't buy this. I don't see my classmates much. It's not a priority for me.

I feel so blessed to be in St. Joseph's parish. Bishop Mugavero told me that he had asked 12 priests to come here as pastor and all of them turned it down. He told me the problems of the parish and I said to him, "If you need me, I'm ready." It turned out that coming to St. Joseph's has been one of the greatest blessings of my life.

First of all, the people, the people are so wonderful. Secondly, I can use my skills here. I can use my mechanical skills as well as my people skills. I can rebuild a boiler and I can counsel a teenager. In another parish I might be more restricted. Thirdly, I can work, like Jesus, with the outcasts of our society.

As I said before, if I could (and I know I can not), I would change the name of the parish to Molokai, the refuge for our modern lepers, immigrants accused of breaking the law. I am free here. There is no one telling me what I can and what I can not do.

I can do my sports programs here. I can do floor hockey in the basement and baseball and volleyball in the large yard; boys and girls playing together in good healthy competition. It's great!

With all this I know I must find the time to pray and pray every day. Early mornings are my best times. I'm usually up by 5: 00 or 5:30 in the morning. Mass is at 8:30. So I save the first part of every day for prayer, silent prayer, meditation.

I go to the chapel in the rectory and pray before the Blessed Sacrament. I do not allow anything or anyone to interfere with this time before the Blessed Sacrament. When I go on retreat, I like to stay by myself. Directed retreats are not for me. I get away for at least one weekly retreat each year.

I'm a voracious reader. I'll finish two or three books a week. I love history. I read mostly history but I'll read a novel every now and then. I read history so we won't make the same mistakes we made in the past, as they say. I read books on the Church. I just finished the Jimmy Breslin book. He took us over the coals. I never knew some of the things he has in this book. It was depressing for me, especially his treatment of the bishops and Murphy's Mansion in Rockville Centre.

Note: Bob was recently assigned to Sacred Heart Parish where he will now face new challenges while continuing his work as an immigration lawyer.

CHAPTER SIXTEEN

REV. JAMES E. SULLIVAN

PRIEST, COUNSELOR, WRITER, REFORMER

I recently celebrated the 60th anniversary of my ordination to the priesthood. Let me tell you a little bit (not the whole thing, of course) about these 60 years.

My first 17 years were in Our Lady of Angels parish in Bay Ridge, Brooklyn. It was a great parish. We had seven priests working in the parish, the pastor and six assistants. We had 2,500 children in the school. We had 35 Sisters of Charity teaching in the school. We had seven Franciscan Brothers teaching the boys in the upper grades. It was a very busy parish. They were very happy years. Then I was transferred to Nativity parish.

I stayed there only one year. The pastor was impossible. I requested a transfer and I was sent to St. Mark's in Sheepshead Bay where I stayed for four years.

While I was in our Lady of Angels I realized that I needed more professional help, if I was to be an effective counselor for people. I had already figured out that most people who came to the rectory with "problems" were not looking for instant solutions. They were looking for someone to listen to them. I enrolled in a counseling program at Iona College. I went to Iona one day a week for four years and received a Master's Degree in counseling.

The years at St. Mark's were very busy years as I began to counsel priests and sisters many hours each day along with my regular parish duties. It was becoming overwhelming.

I realized that the diocese needed a counseling center. I went to see Bishop McEntegart. I made a list of 80 clients, no names just the designation of priest, brother or sister. I wrote their age and their presenting problem, their real problem, the cost of counseling and the results. The bishop was amazed to see this data. (In those days you could still go to a bishop and present your problems.) He gave me permission to start a counseling center, which I named The Religious Consultation Center.

Originally, I wanted to have two centers, one in Brooklyn (Kings County) and one in Queens County but Bishop McEntegart gave me permission for only one to start. I rented space in the Williamsburg Bank building and eventually we had four full-time counselors, two priests and two sisters. Each of us had a Masters in counseling plus three years of our own psychoanalysis so we would not project our own problems on our clients. We had two part-time psychiatrists who could prescribe medication for those who needed it and one part-time psychologist to provide supervision for the counselors and provide an official diagnosis of the clients for insurance purposes. I was proud to be the founder and director of the project.

We were there in the Williamsburg Bank building for 17 years. They kept raising the rent and eventually we had to look for other space. We looked all over, former convents, former Catholic schools, any place where we could set up an office. Finally we found that this house in which we are now sitting was for sale. I gave to Betty Gateley all of the savings I had from the royalties on the books I had written. She used it for a down payment. It turned out that our mortgage payments were less than the rent we had been paying. We paid off the mortgage in five years. Betty owned the house and she used the rent to pay the mortgage. When she died, she left it to me.

During the 26 years of work in the counseling center both in Brooklyn and here we worked with 496 priests in the surrounding dioceses and 25 religious orders. We worked with over 1,500 sisters and brothers. Of the priests, 49 had to leave the active ministry because they fell in love and wanted to get married. Forty-eight were good, wonderful priests, loved by their people. It was a shame they had to leave the priesthood.

I have written a great deal on mandatory celibacy and its effects on priests and its role as the primary cause of the priest shortage. One of my articles is entitled, "Celibacy – The Vatican's Sacred Cow." It has generated a great deal of discussion. What do I mean by this? In what way is celibacy a "sacred cow" for the Vatican?

Celibacy is a "sacred cow" for the Vatican because they hold on to it even though it is so clear that it is ruining the priesthood. World wide over 125,000 priests have left to marry. Seminary enrollment has dropped dramatically. We were a class of 36. Now they are ordaining two or three each year. Priests are getting older. They are being asked to delay retirement until they are 75. They are being asked to cover more than one parish. In Brooklyn, 40 or 50 parishes have only one priest. Yet Rome will not listen to requests to make celibacy optional rather than mandatory.

I have written: "There will be difficulties, of course, when celibacy is made optional – such as necessary changes in housing arrangements, possible break-ups in clerical marriages, harmonizing a two-tiered clergy, etc. The Church will have to face them. However, none of these difficulties is insurmountable and certainly none of them can cause as much harm to the priesthood or to the Church as mandatory celibacy has done. And the benefits that will come to the Church from allowing priests to marry, ordaining married deacons, welcoming married priests back to active ministry, and eventually ordaining women, will be like the effects of a blood transfusion on a pale anemic priesthood"! These are my words.

I know that a married priesthood will bring some problems such as the ones I mentioned there. But optional celibacy will attract men who are more psychosexually mature and less of a haven for homosexual men. Not that some homosexual men can not make good priests. They do. But in the sexual abuse crisis we are now facing, 85% of the victims have been boys. A healthy heterosexual man would never be attracted sexually to a young boy.

I do not hear any of our church leaders asking the big questions: Why have so many left the priesthood? Why are we attracting so few? Why are so many of those who are applying to the seminary homosexuals and in many cases authoritarian?

It kills me that the Vatican seems to have lost its priorities. The supreme law is the salvation of souls (salus animarum) which is much more important than any man-made or church law such as mandatory celibacy. And it is the laity that is suffering.

I published an article in U.S Catholic in December of 2001 entitled "Don't give the priest shortage the silent treatment." In this article I made it clear that I think mandatory celibacy is the primary reason for the priest shortage today. This doesn't come off the top of my head but from the many years I spent working with priests in the Religious Consultation Center. Our conclusion at the Center was that very few priests had the charism of celibacy. For most priests, celibacy was not a gift but a burden and a constant struggle. Many priests had clandestine sexual relationships with women. This resulted in serious feelings of guilt, all of which would not have occurred if priests were allowed to marry.

Along with writing, I've been active in the movement for optional celibacy.

I sent a petition, signed by hundreds of people, to Benedict XVI, requesting "Your Holiness to urge the upcoming International Synod on the Eucharist to make celibacy for our diocesan priests optional rather than mandatory , and to allow our many married priests to return to active ministry." I wrote a letter to each bishop in the United States asking them to sign the petition. A few did. All this was done under the title Save our Sacraments (SOS).

Some well known leaders in the Church such as Thomas Merton, Cardinal Suenens, and Teilhard de Chardin had close relationships with particular women. I think these relationships supported their priesthood. In fact, the healthiest priests we worked with at the

Consultation Center had good relationships with a woman.
Sometimes these relationships became sexual, other times these relationships remained celibate. But the relationships always remained
helpful for the priest as well as the woman. I can speak from experience that my relationships with women have supported my commitment to the priesthood.

My first few years at the Consultation Center were extremely lonely for me. I was listening to people's problems all day. I had some priest
friends and we played golf once a week. If I tried to talk about any
problems at the Center or any problems in the Church they'd say,
"Give us a break, Jimmy. This is our day off." So it was a very lonely
time for me. When Betty Gateley came to work in the Center, she
was excellent, filled a great need. She was a good listener. Both she and
Tom Mannion were the best listeners I've know. I began to get my
loneliness under control because I had two people who understood me
and with whom I could talk about what was on my mind. So the relationship with Betty was good for me and for my priesthood. I knew
this from my own experience.

I have a close relationship with Cathy (Kelly). She is a nurse and
she has been taking care of me for these past seven years, since I've had
the cancer. She's a wonderful woman. She had been married to a priest
for 14 years. When he died and she heard that I was dying of cancer,
she volunteered to take care of me. As you see, I didn't die. She has
been a God-send to me. I don't know what I would have done without
her. She has her rooms upstairs and I have my rooms for sleeping and
reading and writing downstairs. We eat downstairs. It has worked out
fine. (I hope she feels the same way). I am able to say Mass almost
every day. This was her house and when she wanted to sell, Betty
bought it in the name of the Religious Consultation Center. Things
that go around, come around, don't they?

Besides writing on mandatory celibacy, I've written and spoken frequently on my concept of "holiness." For me holiness is simply taking on Jesus Christ.

I love the Gospels, the Acts of the Apostles and the Epistles. I have written two books of meditations on them. I still use them for morning meditation. I love the ideals and the way of life that Jesus preached and lived, his courage in fighting the leaders of his day. (They were so hypercritical, placing burdens on others but not on themselves.) His gentleness with people. His kindness towards women, in an age when women were considered inferior. The imitation of Christ, it seems to me, is the ideal for all priests and for all followers of Christ. I would love it to be my ideal.

When all is said and done, I'm still hopeful. Hopeful for the Church, hopeful for the priesthood.

As the Vatican remains silent about all the real problems in the Church, I think we are going to go down, down in numbers, down in influence. I have hope, as Karl Rahner said, that a remnant will remain faithful like the remnant of Israel that returned to Jerusalem after the Babylonian captivity. Rahner feels there will be a remnant of true believers in the Church that will eventually revitalize it. But first we must go through a period of pain and purification. It has already started.

The source of my hope is Jesus. It is the Gospels, it is the whole of the New Testament including The Acts of the Apostles and the Letters of Paul as we meet disciples like Barnabas, Timothy, Peter and of course, Jesus himself. I love poring over the Gospels and the Acts of the Apostles. This is my source of hope and it's a good one.

Father Jimmy Sullivan died December 13, 2006.

CHAPTER SEVENTEEN

SUMMARY AND CONCLUSIONS

HIDDEN HOLINESS: VOICES OF PRIESTS

F rom interviews and other informal meetings over a year's time, I will summarize and draw conclusions in the following six areas:

- Changes in the relationship of priest to bishop
- Celibacy
- The priesthood, becoming an isolated profession
- Prayerfulness and simplicity of life
- The effects of the Priest-Worker Movement
- The parish

CHANGES IN THE RELATIONSHIP OF PRIEST TO BISHOP

It is remarkable to see the changes that have taken place in the relationship between the 15 priests who participated in the study and their bishops. Bishop Frank Mugavero had been the Director of Catholic Charities in the Diocese of Brooklyn before succeeding Bryan McEntegart as bishop and he brought the sensitivity of a social worker into the episcopacy. He encouraged and supported the experimental parish, Our Lady of the Presentation, in Brownsville that had begun under Bishop McEntegart. As priests moved from rectories to apartments, from parish work to factory work, from celibacy to marriage, Bishop Mugavero continued to support them.

He appointed Father Ed Burke to be the coordinator of the work of the priests who participated in the experimental parish. The bishop was interested in the work of the priests and he wanted to be kept informed about their ministries. He was very human. He could usually be found on a Friday night playing cards in his apartment with his closest friends and classmates. When he would visit Transfiguration parish and speak to Bryan Karvelis he would always ask for John Mulhern, a married priest, who worked closely with Father Karvelis for many years. But the Bishop never asked too many questions. He was happy to hear that John was feeling well. And they went on to other topics. He was very sensitive.

When the East Brooklyn Congregations needed seed money to start on what would eventually be the building of more than 3,000 single-family homes, John Powis went to Bishop Mugavero and reported back that the Bishop had agreed to lend EBC seed money to start the housing project. All the money with interest has been paid back to the diocese. Bishop Mugavero was respected and loved by the priests of the Diocese of Brooklyn.

One day, Bishop McEntegart, before he retired, called for a meeting of all the priests involved in the experimental parish. The fear was that he was not going to support the life style of the priests and would order them to return to rectories and abandon apartment living. No such thing occurred. He made it clear that he supported the experimental parish. He did not order the priests to leave the apartments where they were living. He did not cut back on any of their freedoms. He only wanted to know (tongue in cheek) how he could justify his position to their mothers if their priest-sons should become seriously ill. He told the priests (with a smile), "don't get sick."

It seems appropriate to show similarities between Emmanuel Cardinal Suhard of Paris and Bishops Bryan McEntegart and Francis Mugavero of Brooklyn. All three saw that new approaches must be tried because the French Church was losing the working class and the New York City Church was losing the recent immigrants and the poor. Outreach was necessary both in France and in New York. The point is that both the Worker-Priest movement and the experimental parish in Brownsville had the support and encouragement of their local bishops. The priests in French factories and the priests ringing doorbells in a housing project in Brownsille knew they had the backing of a Cardinal Suhard or a Bishop Mugavero or a Bishop McEntegart. The priests reaching out to immigrants and the poor in the inner city today need the same kind of support from their bishops. Are they getting it?

It is clear in these examples that there was, at one time, a strong bond between father (the bishop) and his son (the priest). This bond has been severely damaged by what is called the Dallas Charter written by the bishops and distributed at their Episcopal meeting in Dallas, Texas in 2002. In this document the bishops put full blame on priests for the sexual abuse scandal in the Church and developed the "one strike and you're out" policy. No bishop is blamed for poor management in handling the sexual abuse cases in his diocese. No bishop is censured by his fellow bishops for moving known sex offenders from one parish to another.

The priests interviewed are angry about this. They feel that if their bishop calls them to a meeting, perhaps they should bring a lawyer with them. They feel the bond between priest and bishop has been broken. Priests no longer see their bishop as "father" but as "middle manager" whose first concern is to save himself and his job. As Joe Nugent put it, "The bishops have turned their backs on all of us. The bond that once existed between the priests and their bishop has been broken."

Most of the priests interviewed feel they can no longer trust their bishop. They feel that, as a group, bishops are more interested in looking good in Rome than in being good shepherds at home. A dramatic change in the relationship of priest to bishop has taken place in the last five years and it is a significant change.

It would be worthwhile to contrast Richard Smith with Jim Richardson who feels a great deal of support and interest from his new Archbishop Henry Mansell, as well as from his Auxiliary Bishop Peter Rosazza.

At ordination time, the priest about to be ordained places his hands within the hands of the ordaining bishop and promises obedience. It is a very tender moment. It is a symbolic act that might take place between an aging father and his young son. It is an act of love and respect. At a meeting of priests in New York, Msgr. William Varvaro of Brooklyn cautioned the priests not to go to any meeting with the bishop unless they bring a lawyer with them for counsel and advice. That's how far things have come, from a symbol of love and respect at the time of ordination to caution and fear today. The Dallas Charter is largely responsible for damaging the once filial relationship between bishop and priest.

The key word is dialogue. Bishops have to be willing to talk to their priests, both in groups, large and small, and individually. This dialogue must be free and open, not carefully screened. Priests should be able to speak their minds without fear of reprisals. The bishop himself, not his delegate, should be present for these sessions and must not only listen but respond to the concerns expressed by his priests. Priests must be prepared to listen to the viewpoints of their bishop. Msgr Phillip Murnion, a few days before his death, said that three things are necessary in the Church today, "Dialogue, Dialogue, Dialogue."

CELIBACY

Much to my surprise, in spite of the loneliness that comes from living without a spouse, all of the priests said "yes" celibacy had worked for them. However they all also said "no" it should not be mandated for the entire Church. Many felt that since their lives were so hectic and busy, it would not be fair to a woman to be married to such a person. They also admitted that celibacy was the only way of life they had ever known. They were basically happy living as celibates but felt that mandating this way of life for all priests coupled with living alone, does not make the priesthood attractive to young men today. This is especially true as the image of the priest in the community has been tarnished by the sex abuse scandals.

Some of the priests admitted that they are lonely at times, but we are all lonely at times, celibates as well as married people. We do not choose to be lonely. It is part of the human condition. It all depends on how we deal with our loneliness. We can try to drink it to death and become bitter or we can use it to better realize that we all need friends and intimacy and healthy relationships in our lives.

The priests were divided on the question of availability. Some felt that without the need to provide for a wife and children, a celibate priest would be more available to the people in the parish than a married priest would be. Others felt strongly that marital status was not the issue. It all depends on how we use our time, for self or for others. It is easy for celibate priests to adapt a "bachelor mentality" and become self-centered so that everything must be done their way and on their time or not done at all.

All of the priests acknowledged that celibacy is a charism, a gift, an individual personal decision that can not be mandated. Obviously, the priests interviewed had this gift and were using it well. John Mulhern does not have the gift of celibacy but has many other gifts that he is using well. For him the gifts of compassion, of relating well to others, of feeling another's pain are the important gifts, not marital status. Jack Peyton admits that his ministry might have been more effective if he were married and had some feedback on how he was doing.

All of the priests supported optional celibacy for diocesan priests. They looked forward to the day when priests could be celibate or married, with each bringing his special gifts to ministry for building up the kingdom of God. Married priests would not be considered less priestly and celibate priests would not be considered less manly.

Jim Sullivan, who directed the Religious Consultation Center for 26 years and counseled hundreds of priests, has a unique perspective on celibacy. It is a perspective that does not come off the top of his head but from many years of working with priests. For him celibacy is the primary source of the priest shortage. He writes, "Our conclusion at the Center was that very few priests had the charism of celibacy. For most priests, celibacy was not a gift but a burden and a constant struggle."

While bishops may be comforted in knowing that the priests interviewed feel that celibacy has worked for them personally, bishops must also recognize that priests feel overworked. They feel that many of their brother priests are discouraged and they themselves are strongly in favor of optional celibacy for the diocesan priesthood.

Bishops with "pastoral hearts," who see that they can not adequately staff all of their parishes, must speak out in favor of optional celibacy, no matter how unpopular that might be in Rome. However, considering the quality of our bishops and their general lack of leadership and courage, this is unlikely to happen. What is more likely to happen is that bishops will say nothing, keep things as they are, continue to close or merge parishes and do nothing to lessen the burden on those priests who are pastors of more than one parish and feel trapped in a ministry they had not anticipated.

Some bishops are beginning to prepare for "Priestless Sundays" by the development of Lay Institutes. The purpose of these Lay Institutes is to train the baptized, including deacons and religious women as well as the laity, on how to run a parish in the absence of a full-time priest. It is interesting that because bishops would not take the initiative to advocate optional celibacy, they are forced to take the more radical step of allowing the baptized to administer the parish, preach and celebrate some of the sacraments. The future of the Church does not lie in a male, celibate priesthood but in the training of its most spiritual and educated people to run parishes and do the pastoral work.

THE PRIESTHOOD, BECOMING AN ISOLATED PROFESSION

Msgr. Donald Cozzens, in his book, *The Changing Face of the Priesthood* said the priesthood is becoming a "gay profession." This may or may not be true. It is hard to prove. On the other hand it is easy to prove that the priesthood is becoming an "isolated profession." It is one of the effects of the priest shortage. To put it simply, more and more priests are living alone.

Even though diocesan priests were never trained to work or live in community, when there were four or five men living in the same rectory there was always the chance that priests could work together on various projects and some might even become friends. Now as more and more priests live alone, this sharing and these friendships are no longer possible.

What came across clearly in the interviews with the priests was that they were either living alone now or will be living alone soon. Some priests are living alone in very large rectories. Jim Richardson commented, "My rectory is a very large building with three floors and 12-foot ceilings. It has 23 rooms. It was made for four or five priests with each priest having a suite of rooms. It is clearly too big for me. On most nights I am the only one sleeping there. Some kids will ask me, "Do you live in that big house all by yourself?"

Bob Vitaglione and Frank Shannon are in similar situations— that is living alone in large rectories that were built to house five or six priests. Frank said that when he was ordained he never thought he'd be living alone in a large rectory, but he is.

Men do not enter a diocesan seminary to live the solitary life of a hermit. Also, living alone brings temptations of all kinds, such as opportunities for excessive drinking or inappropriate relationships that might not be present if there were another person in the house to whom the priest is accountable. It is usually not a good idea to be accountable to no one. A priest living alone must rely on a solid spiritual life, close friends and a good working relationship with those men and women working in the rectory.

It is basic theology that grace does not destroy nature but builds on nature. For most people, to live alone all the time is not healthy. Superiors of religious orders know this well. They rarely allow their members to live alone. If bishops do not learn this lesson quickly, they will soon be faced with the problems described below.

An article in America magazine pointed out that Catholic chaplains in the military, who are living alone in their own homes, off base, are a minority of the total number of chaplains. Yet these Catholic chaplains commit a greater percentage of sexual crimes leading to dismissal from the military than do their Protestant counterparts, who form the majority of chaplains. Why? Because Catholic priests are more perverted than Protestant ministers? No. The simple reason is that living alone in a house, off base, offers greater opportunities for bad judgments than if there were other persons in the house to whom one is accountable. As bishops allow more and more of their priests to live alone, they will soon be facing the same problems as superiors of Catholic chaplains in the military are facing.

The solution may be in the formation of "communal rectories" that, at least, offer the opportunities for priests in a particular region to live, eat and plan together. So instead of three priests living alone in three different rectories, they would live in one rectory and two of them would "commute" to work.

PRAYERFULNESS AND SIMPLICITY OF LIFE

PRAYERFULNESS

It was impressive to discover that all of the priests participating in this study are men of prayer or men who are striving to be prayerful. Three of those interviewed are active in a priest Fraternity of Charles de Foucauld which calls on its members to spend an hour each day in prayer before the Blessed Sacrament and to get away each month for a "Day of Desert."

Not all the priests interviewed for this study follow the spirituality of Charles de Foucauld but all are searching to make time for prayer in spite of leading busy, hectic life styles. Here are some examples:

Bob Vitaglione gets up by 5:30 in the morning so he has about three hours for prayer before the 8:30 Mass that he celebrates each day. Also, he gets away for at least one week retreat each year. Joe Nugent says the rosary and some of the Divine Office each day as well as spending some time in prayer before the Blessed Sacrament. For Andy Connolly prayer is a time of reflection when he makes sure that in his work he is building the kingdom of God and not his own kingdom.

All of the priests interviewed were trying to make a holy hour each day or at least to make some time each day to be alone with the Lord. Most priests found the time before Mass in the morning to be the time with the fewest interruptions and therefore the time most conducive to prayer. Some read parts of the Divine Office each day, others did not.

Bishops can take comfort in knowing that their priests are men of prayer. They might welcome opportunities to pray with their priests on a regular basis. We have already seen that differences between priests and bishops are rooted in fear, and sometimes in different theological perspectives. Joining each other in prayer would help to build respect and a better understanding between priest and bishop.

SIMPLICITY OF LIFE

When talking about poverty and simplicity of life, stronger feelings emerged than I had anticipated. The priests were upset that "everyone talks about celibacy. No one talks about poverty. Could it be that we are better at being chaste than we are in being poor?" asked one priest with a smile.

The priests interviewed seem to have few possessions outside of a car, a computer and many books. Frank Shannon and John Powis do not even own a car. Frank rides his bike through the parish. He says, "I try to live a simple life not because I am heroic but because it fits into my personality and my way of life. I am not impressed with any priest who buys a big, expensive car. Give me my bike and let me be."

John Powis puts it this way, "I try to spend as little as possible on myself. I don't have a savings account and I don't own a car."

Bryan Karvelis has another view of poverty which is very much influenced by his commitment to the spirituality of Brother Charles de Foucauld. For Bryan poverty means that you don't keep anything that would separate you from the poorest of the people you serve and among whom you live. The emphasis is being with the poor and living as the poor, being a little brother to them. So when Bryan was living with the 25 or 30 men in the rectory, he would not use the air conditioner in his room as long as the other men did not have an air conditioner in their rooms.

Andy Connolly expressed what other priests also said that it isn't just priests who are called to live a simple life style. It is the vocation of all Christians to be poor.

Most of the priests interviewed agreed that leading a simple life was important for two reasons. First, because they were struggling to follow Jesus who was poor and secondly because they were working with poor people. For these priests, poverty had to do with attachments. In order to be attached to God they had to be free of any attachment to people or things. Poverty has to do with the recognition that we need God more than we need any person or thing. Simplicity of life, like celibacy, is a daily struggle.

It was easy to see the influence of Dorothy Day and the Catholic Worker Movement on many of the priests. Some of them mention her by name. She saw radical voluntary poverty as a charism, a sign that we do not have here a lasting dwelling. Those who have this charism serve as a sign to all that the following of Jesus requires a simple life style. All of the priests interviewed lived simply and were very sensitive that they be seen by their people as, if not poor, at least as not having a lot of luxuries.

THE EFFECTS OF THE WORKER-PRIEST MOVEMENT

As I listened to the voices of men trying to articulate what their lives have been all about, I began to see similarities between those priests who worked in the experimental parish in Brownsville in the 60's and the 70's and those priests who were Worker–Priests in France (1948 – 1954).

• Both saw their work as a "mission."

• Both not only worked with the poor but lived with the poor in apartments rather than in rectories.

- Both identified with the struggles of the poor and marched with them and demonstrated with them.

- Both saw their work as experimental, as new ways of being priests among the marginalized of society.

The Worker–Priest movement lasted only a few years, but it had a great influence in the Catholic world outside of France. It received frequent and favorable articles in the *The New York Times* and *Newsweek*. Stories about the Worker-Priests appeared often in *America* and *Commonweal*. It influenced Dorothy Day and Peter Maurin at the Catholic Worker. As Oscar Arnal wrote in *Priests in Working Class Blue,* "Whether in France or elsewhere the worker-priests have left their mark, and they continue to do so. They have captured the hearts and vision of a wider public and their living presence has spawned a multitude of parallel missionary forms within the working class and among the poor." So it is not surprising that the small cadre of priests in Brownsville, while not seeing themselves exactly as worker-priests, adapted much of the vocabulary and strategies of the worker-priests in their alternative ministries. Two of the Brooklyn priests took jobs and went to work. Tony Equale worked in a factory and Donald Kenna worked in Con Edison while remaining a parish priest and a pastor.

The worker-priests used such words as "incarnation," "presence," "witness," and "immersion" to explain their mission to the working class. The priests interviewed who had worked in the experimental parish in Brownsville or were influenced by the worker-priests, used similar language such as: "We wanted to be like Jesus who lived with the people," "You have to be with the people so their struggles become your struggles." "Slowly, with God's grace, I was developing a commitment to live with the poor and join in their struggle against the causes of poverty." "I spent all my years on assignment from the diocese in alternative ministries. I lived with two other priests in a slum apartment. I worked in two factories and was very much influenced by the priest-worker movement in France."

Donald Kenna was a Worker-Priest in the 60's, 70's and 80's. For him it was simply a matter of the Gospel. So he worked a "regular job," lived in an apartment, cooked, cleaned, and did laundry for himself, while being pastor of a Church in Brooklyn. It should be noted that Kenna was not able to recruit others to follow him as worker-priests. There was great interest in what he was doing, but unlike France, no movement started in Brooklyn or in the United States.

It is a tribute to Bishops McEntegart and Mugavero who trusted their priests to find new ways of ministering to the poor. This trust continued even as some of the priests living in apartments left the priesthood to marry, as other priests were doing.

There are other bishops who trust their priests. Bishop Paul Bootkoski of the Diocese of Metuchen, New Jersey, is a good example of a bishop who is reaching out to gain the trust of his priests. There are more. We just don't hear their stories.

THE PARISH

The great strength of the Catholic Church has been the loyalty people have shown to their parish and to their parish priests. Even at the height of the sex abuse scandal, most Catholics kept going to Mass and supported their local Church and priests, even as they stopped contributing to the Cardinal's Campaign. There was a time when Catholics identified where they lived by the parish they went to. So people living in Woodside, Queens would say, "I go to St. Sebastians," or "I live in St. Teresa's."

The parish meant a lot more than Mass on Sunday. It meant going to the Catholic school where the sisters taught all the members of the family, playing basketball for the parish teams, going to the parish dances, going to meetings of the CYO (Catholic Youth Organization), boys and girls meeting each other at parish functions and marrying, coming back to baptize children. The parish was the heart and soul of the social life of young Catholics.

All of the priests in this study were or still are parish priests. This is what they were trained to do and this is what they enjoyed doing. They knew the families in their parish and the families knew them. All this is in the process of breaking down or as John Gildea puts it, "We are downsizing." Catholic schools are merging. Convents, built to house 10 to 12 sisters, now have one or two living there.

Priests are assigned to cover two or three parishes and they have to make it clear to their parishioners that they can not provide the same level of service that four or five priests could provide in the past. In merged parishes priests can cover the Masses but pastoral work suffers.

Fr. John Gildea reports that in the area of Brooklyn where he is now stationed there are two priests where there used to be ten and one parish where there used to be three. The parish structure is breaking down and a "filling station" mentality is replacing the "family" mentality.

When Frank Shannon was in Blessed Sacrament parish with four priests he was able to spend a great deal of time in the parish gym getting to know the youth of the parish. Now as the only priest in the parish, he can not afford the time to hang out with the parish youth.

The parish is still the place where people meet the Church. If the parishes become irrelevant to youth and to families, the Church will become irrelevant.

Thomas A. McCabe